TERRORISM

TERRORISM

ITS GOALS
ITS TARGETS
ITS METHODS

THE SOLUTIONS

MICHAEL CONNOR

PALADIN PRESS
BOULDER, COLORADO

TERRORISM
its goals, its targets, its methods
THE SOLUTIONS
by Michael Connor

ISBN 0-87364-404-2
Printed in the United States of America

Published by Paladin Press, a division of
Paladin Enterprises, Inc., P.O. Box 1307,
Boulder, Colorado 80306, USA.
(303) 443-7250

Direct inquiries and/or orders to the above address.

Contents

International revolutionary forces will soon meet to map a joint strategy for a war against the United States.

Abu Abbas
Palestine Liberation Front
December 1985

Preface

"Terrorism" and "terrorist" are, of course, arbitrary labels, which can be employed or ignored as befits the viewpoint of the individual. Consequently, the efforts of a group to further its objectives through fear will only be considered terrorist if you do not happen to agree with them. If you do, they become, thanks to the action of the great god Semantics, "freedom fighters" or "liberators."

Many, however, will not make this interpretation themselves. Instead they join the ranks of others before them who have lost their clarity of judgment, their lives, or their freedom through the process of persuasion.

The so-called terrorist may be politically motivated, but then again he may not be. He may be driven by a desire to avenge some historical injustice, or he may be a religious fanatic. He may be insane, or he may be as sane as you or I. He may be a simple criminal seeking to legitimize his crimes in the name of ideology; he may be intent on destruction or content with disruption. *He* may even be a *she*.

Given even this condensed range of motivations, the spectrum of possible targets for terrorist action is a broad one. Just what or who are those targets likely to be, and why? How might the terrorist achieve his aims? These are the questions we will examine here.

Honi soit qui mal y pense.

(Shamed be he who thinks evil of it.)

1

Terrorism: A Definition

It is generally accepted that the terms *terrorism* and *terrorist* as they are used today were born of the *regime de la terreur,* or Reign of Terror (1793–1794) in revolutionary France.

At that time enemies of the revolution, as defined by the Robespierre council on an increasingly arbitrary basis, faced arrest, imprisonment, and death by guillotine. Initially, the targets of this terror were aristocrats, but Robespierre's frantic efforts to eliminate any and every possible threat to the revolution gradually drew him to look closer at hand for "enemies." Even those supportive of the revolution, albeit more moderately, were eventually attacked.

It was inevitable that before too long, potential victims, driven by a desire to kill before being themselves killed, decided upon pre-emptive action. On July 27, 1794, Robespierre and his clique were murdered. The Reign of Terror, which had seen some four hundred thousand "suspects" (including many children and women) imprisoned and many more thousands executed, ended.

From those whose status could be determined, less than 40 percent of those executed in 1793 and 1974 were found to be aristocrats. In view of these figures, it would be possible to argue that terrorism is a systematic application of terror, instilled and reinforced by continual murders, used to establish and maintain a political system. Indeed, definitions such as this are still offered from time to time by commentators on the phenomenon. Today, however, such a definition will not find wide and general acceptance as it does not differentiate *terrorism* from other acts of aggression in which there is a terror component. Though such a component exists, it is not the perpetrator's primary objective.

In a conventional war, for example, terror is present for the most part only as a natural by-product of straightforward combat. Targets are chosen with a view to the rapid elimination of the enemy and/or the destruction or disruption of its command, control, communication, support, and supply networks. Victory is decided by force of numbers, skill at arms, weapons superiority, strategy and tactics, or a combination of all such factors. A point may be reached at which one of the protagonists concludes that victory is possible, but that the cost is too great; or one side may become so demoralized that it decides to surrender or abandon the war effort.

Fear or terror is not the determining factor in such conflicts. If it *were* the fundamental reason for defeat, it would follow that disproportionately intense fear had been generated by enemy attacks; it would imply that a higher percentage of the defeated army had been frightened than physically injured.

Those frightened but not physically injured are the true victims of terrorism. Other casualties may be classified according to the mode by which the victims met their death. Our working definition of terrorism therefore might better be: the use and/or threat of repeated violence, in support of or in opposition to some authority, where violence is employed to induce fear of similar attack in as many non-immediate victims as possible so that those so threatened will accept and comply with the demands of the terrorists. A wordy definition, but by necessity so.

Within this definition we find scope to describe the

actions of terrorists acting upon a variety of motives; at the same time, the definition remains neutral with regard to the great variety of individual traits which characterize particular groups. Thus we can refer to political terrorism, revolutionary terrorism, state terrorism, and so on. This, to my mind, is far more satisfactory and realistic than suggesting a particular type of motivation as part of the definition of terrorism. One cannot even say that all terrorism is politically motivated.

The emplacement of an incendiary device in a department store or the poisoning of selected foodstuffs on the shelves by "animal rights" groups (a type of event that is becoming more frequent, especially in Europe) are acts calculated to induce fear and anxiety in a wide number of people, a far larger number of people than are likely to be injured by the acts themselves. The perpetrators of the act believe that by such means commercial concerns can be coerced into abandoning product-testing on animals, battery-farming methods, or other such uses of animals. Their acts are most definitely acts of terrorism, but are not politically motivated.

Our definition of terrorism is also deliberately constructed to exclude acts of violence in which the terror component is incidental or secondary to some other primary objective. The death of an eminent politician, for example, may be the goal of an extremist group that wishes to deprive the electorate of his particular quality of leadership; or he may be about to introduce some item of legislation which will seriously counter the group's aims. That such a murder would generate fear is, in this instance, of secondary importance to the actual liquidation of the individual. The perpetrators would more likely be called "murderers" or "assassins" than terrorist.

Similarly, repeated incidents of violence at a football match involving attacks by supporters of one team against supporters of another, or even against passers-by in the street outside the stadium, can lead to the generation of such fear among local inhabitants that they sell out and move away or at least take care to avoid the area whenever a match is being played. We could not call the offenders here "terrorists," however, since they are not attempting to persuade others to accept some view or demand. The terror effect is, again, incidental.

On the other hand, if the extremist group that assassinated a leading politician were also to issue a statement of demands and threaten that more politicians and even non-government targets would be attacked if demands were not met, then it would be realistic to label the group "terrorists."

It is clear that categorizing someone as a terrorist as defined herein does not preclude also categorizing that same person as a madman, guerrilla, ideologist, or a revolutionary. A grocer who races hot rods on weekends is a racing driver. He does not, however, stop being a grocer.

The fact that to some, members of the IRA (Irish Republican Army), PLO (Palestine Liberation Organization), or ETA (Euzkadi Ta Azkatasuna) are "freedom fighters," while to others they remain "terrorists," proves only that without recourse to some established definitional parameters such labels are purely a matter of moral value judgment. If the person making the judgment does not agree with the objectives of the group perpetrating the violence, the latter is described (with very few exceptions) as "terrorist." The group thus categorized denies this, of course, and claims to be a "national liberation army," a "workers army," or whatever. The inference is that a terrorist group has no legitimacy and that its aims, therefore, have no validity. "Terrorist" becomes a term of derogation.

Once we accept, however, that terrorism is a technique—nothing more and nothing less—we can apply the term sensibly without running afoul of various moral beliefs and socio-political ideologies. The operatives of the PLO are terrorists, but that does not in itself mean that their aims and objectives are without validity. IRA members can be described as freedom fighters, but they must also accept the terrorist label.

Obviously it is easier for one to perceive a long-established, freely elected regime as legitimate than it is to accept that a handful of individuals with views significantly different from those of the majority might deserve the same classification. This is especially so if the methods used by the handful of individuals provoke moral indignation by being actions traditionally reserved for use in wartime against a sanctioned target—"the enemy." When an indiscriminate "enemy" label is applied to those not actually supportive of an aggressor's objective, the situation becomes far more disturbing, more so because the aggressors frequently "fight dirty." They wear no uniform to indicate their presence and employ weapons that they need not personally fire or activate (mail bombs, time bombs, etc.). Thus the "fairness" factor is removed, leaving us frequently with an unknown aggressor killing unknown victims for a reason which will not be made clear until after the event.

In the period from 1939 to 1945, the actions of an American who had succeeded in placing a bomb in some important government building in West Germany, thereby killing several Nazi chiefs, would have been applauded almost universally as "a brave and heroic deed." If the same sequence of events were repeated today, however, the perpetrator would be almost universally condemned as a terrorist or murderer. The only difference, of course, is that no group or nation—other than minority extremist groups—is officially at war with West Germany and thus the action is difficult to justify.

There will always be some "bottom-line" considerations, of course, even when the targets are acceptable "enemies" in the eyes of many onlookers. Strikes against Soviet-backed regimes, for example, find more favor among Western observers, even when such strikes are plainly definable as terrorist, because the Soviets are our accepted Cold-War enemies. But if the nature of the assault transgresses certain unwritten but widely accepted boundaries of "decency" or "fair play," then condemnation is more neutrally applied. The downing of a Soviet helicopter gunship by elements of the Afghanistan Mujahadeen, for example, is interpreted by all (save for supporters of the Soviets) to be more acceptable than the downing of a civilian airliner by the PLO. The deliberate slaughter of armed soldiers in an ambush is more easily accepted than is the slaughter of small children.

In descending order of quality or "fair game," then, we might list: 1) military personnel, 2) government officials, and 3) civilians unconnected in any way with the continuance of the policy against which the terrorist is fighting. This same (deliberately abbreviated) list might constitute the basis of a target selection for almost any military offensive. A true terrorist group, on the other hand, might consider the following order to be more appropriate: 1) civilians unconnected in any way with the continuance of the policy against which the group is fighting, 2) government officials, and 3) military personnel.

The simple fact is that *more* fear and anxiety can be generated by attacks against non-combatants than could be by attacks against strictly military or government targets. Demonstrating to the populace as a whole that the incumbent regime is unable to protect them is generally a far safer technique for the terrorist group than trying to prove that the regime cannot protect itself—which is rarely ever the case. It follows then that the true terror group will frequently have to outrage and cause revulsion in its target audience in order to maintain the required degree of terror. This in itself suggests that unless some way is found to deter future acts of terrorism, the nature of those acts will, indeed, become more terrifying.

2

Why Terrorism?

The belief that terrorism is always a last-resort weapon of the oppressed has long been abandoned in all but the most irrational individuals. Revolutionary groups advocating the introduction of a different political system and nationalist/separatist groups seeking freedom from external control have used terrorism against governments totalitarian/authoritarian and democratic in nature. More importantly, people who, given an opportunity, may have been sympathetic to the cause of a group may have been killed or maimed in its name along with its outspoken opponents.

Terror tactics have indeed been used as a shortcut to circumvent the democratic process, but they have also been employed in this way by those in power to maintain what they see as order. Stalin, Lenin, Hitler, and Idi Amin—via whose State Research Bureau Public Safety Unit some 300,000 people were tortured and murdered[1]—are perhaps the names that spring most readily to mind in this context. The practice of the Soviet government of incarcerating individuals who express dissent in lunatic asylums also certainly falls into this category. This practice must be seen as equivalent to or worse than the actions of terrorist groups proper that have taken and held hostages and later released them physically unharmed. Some would say that the current Soviet regime relies heavily on terrorism to survive.

There is another motivation behind the techniques,

strategies, and aims of terror groups of the nationalist/separatist or political revolutionary variety. There is a great desire for publicity. Many groups confuse sympathy and publicity, of course, and mistakenly assume that one automatically follows the other. Nonetheless, it is obvious that the murder of an American politician in the supposed safety of his own home may be a preferred goal of a terrorist group because it generates more publicity than actions seemingly more directly related to the group's ends. Such an act generates more publicity, for example, than the assassination of a dozen cabinet ministers from a small little-known country. Massive world attention can be brought to focus on a "cause," then, by the simple expedient of killing or kidnapping a few people and issuing a statement explaining why it has been done. Given that personal interpretation will color the views of readers, viewers, and listeners, the terrorist can safely conclude that though many individuals may be disgusted and dismayed by the act, there will be at least some who see it as justified.

The publicity in some cases is not wanted for a cause as such. Sometimes a group will feel that it simply has to publicize its own existence. This may be the case with a new, unsupported group with vague or undefined aims. Examples have been the Black Liberation Army, the Symbionese Liberation Army,[2] and various splinter groups separating from an established organization. The INLA, for example, sought this kind of publicity when it split with the IRA in 1974 over policy differences.[3]

Aside from publicity, then, what else can be achieved by the use of acts producing terror that could not be arrived at simply through more selective violence? Military forces, police, and other professional peace-keeping personnel are difficult to defeat in direct confrontation. They are also more difficult to intimidate by acts of terror than are untrained civilians. Most important, attacks on security forces do not psychologically implicate the general population. Thus terrorist campaigns must include attacks against unsuspecting, unprepared civilians if they are to generate any lasting societal instability. Even the murder of a politician cannot be guaranteed to throw fear into the hearts of all the electorate, for such an attack, while horrific in itself, still indicates that the terrorists are targeting only officials. In truth, the less directly the target has to do with the cause, the greater the terror effect. *Were* terrorists to select only those targets related to their grievances, then everyone not directly related to the perpetration of the offending condition could assume they had nothing to fear. This would mean much less intense general reaction and thus greatly reduced effectiveness.

It is precisely the knowledge that *anyone* might fall victim to the next bomb blast or burst of rifle fire that produces terror. Sometimes this effect is so great that it even reduces the number of potential converts to a cause or frightens part of the existing membership of a group. Hence, for example, the INLA/IRA split. With this effect in mind, terror groups have, from time to time, adopted a more restrained approach.

In 1963 elements of the FALN (Fuerzas Armadas de Liberacion Nacional), a Venezuelan radical group composed of idealists and military officers, launched a campaign to overthrow President Romulo Betancourt. Early efforts at gaining mass support failed, and more extreme measures were called for. Specialized assaults were undertaken with a view to attracting world interest. American oil pipelines and related targets were sabotaged and news of the group spread rapidly. On January 16, 1963, a new strategy emerged when the group raided an exhibition of French art and stole several priceless masterpieces. They returned them less than a week later. On August 24, 1963, the same group kidnapped a high-ranking administrator from the United States embassy. Some ten days later, amid tremendous publicity and to the amazement of many, he was released—with boot polish in his hair. Sadly, within days of this action, the FALN launched a series of vicious attacks against the Venezuelan security forces, and their bizarre but effective theatrical approach deteriorated into bloody warfare. Ultimately the campaign achieved little, and in December of the same year the majority of the electorate voted for an unrelated political party. The FALN faded into memory.

The Tupamaros was a Uruguayan terrorist movement, known also as the MLN (Movimiento de Liberacion Nacional). It was founded in the 1960s and remained sporadically active until its demise in 1972. The Tupamaros also took great care in the early stages of their campaign to avoid indiscriminate murder. They raided businesses, banks, shops, and stores. Occasionally they gave away the goods and money thus acquired to workers. They stole documents revealing corruption in high places and published them for the general public. After 1970, however, the actions of the group became more violent and several foreign diplomats were kidnapped and/or killed.[4]

Currently operational terrorist groups often claim that they are selective about their targets, that they avoid indiscriminate violence. In some cases this is true. Even where the target chosen seems irrelevant or to involve totally innocent people, a warning will be given with a view to reducing casualties. Problems arise because those perceived as enemies by the terrorists often appear no more than innocent bystanders to everyone else. Passengers at an airport check-in for a flight to a country against which the terrorists are staging attacks are "legitimate" targets simply because they are using services relating to the enemy regime. This amounts in the mind of the terrorists to cooperation with the enemy. Extreme left-wing groups find it easy to classify all businessmen as legitimate targets because they represent "the evil capitalist system." The fact that such groups often kidnap businessmen and then demand huge (i.e., capitalist-style) ransoms for their release suggests another definition problem.

Indiscriminate – or better, unpredictable–attacks,

then, ensure widespread reaction. Terrorists believe that fear will make the targeted populace put pressure on its government to accept demands or make concessions "so that the attacks will stop." Failing this result, continued assaults will at least provoke increased security measures. Such measures will bring about a reduction in civil liberty, and thus the people will be turned against their leaders. At this point the terrorist group, via its moderate-faced political wing, will be in a position to offer an acceptable alternative.

NOTES

1. Charles Freeman, *Terrorism* (London: Batsford Academic and Educational, 1981), p. 15.

2. Black Liberation Army (BLA), formed from remnants of the Black Panthers. This group indulged in senseless acts of murder, primarily against police officers, both black and white. Active in the early 1970s. The Symbionese Liberation Army (SLA) appeared initially in California in 1973. The name had nothing to do with a tyrant-ruled country, but was defined by the group as meaning "a body of harmony of dissimilar bodies and organisms living in deep and loving harmony and partnership in the best interest of within the body." It comprised no more than a dozen or so criminals, homosexuals, and madmen. The group attained worldwide notoriety after the kidnapping of Patricia Hearst.

3. It is generally accepted that the IRA "old school" favored more discriminate use of violent tactics.

4. Walter Laqueur, *Terrorism* (London: Weidenfield and Nicolson, 1977).

3

Who Becomes a Terrorist?

The popular, and largely accurate, image of today's terrorist is that of a young person. The reasonable explanation for this is simply that terrorist active service requires those qualities of fitness, daring, and strength most often found in the young. Also, an individual close to middle age is far more likely to have come to terms with the injustices and failings of his society and found some alternative way of seeking to alter, remove, avenge, or live with them. Having failed to notice and/or react to them while young, he has probably chosen to ignore them. Middle-aged people are extremely unlikely to respond to a call to arms from activists many years their junior. In addition, there is the terrorist lifestyle itself, which is hardly conducive to a long and healthy existence. In terrorism, however, as in any other field of human endeavor, there are exceptions.

Daniel Curley, member of a nineteenth-century Irish nationalist group, the Invincibles, who in May 1882, butchered Lord Frederick Cavendish and his private secretary, in an attack which was soon to become known as the "Phoenix Park Murders," was hanged for his crime at the age of twenty.[1] Zvonko Busic, hijacker of TWA Flight 335 in September 1976, was thirty,[2] and Oan, leader of the terrorist group involved in the Iranian embassy siege in London in 1980, was twenty-seven.[3] Ali Amor Marzuki, one of the Arab hijackers of Egyptian Boeing 737 on November 23, 1984, was twenty-two.[4] By contrast, Latin American terrorist

Carlos Marighella, author of the "minimanual" on guerrilla warfare, was elected leader of the Brazilian urban guerrilla movement while in his fifties.[5]

Many German and Italian terrorists of the early 1920s were as young as sixteen,[6] and in recent years a similar trend toward violence and martyrdom has re-emerged among teenage members of various Middle Eastern factions. One of the four Palestinians who hijacked the Italian cruise ship *Achille Lauro* in 1985, for example, had to be retried for his crime after it was discovered that he was only seventeen. A six-and-a-half-year sentence had been awarded him before his age was discovered. And in November 1985, a court in Tel Aviv jailed a sixteen-year-old Palestinian for having hidden the bodies of two Israeli teachers whose murders had triggered anti-Arab riots.[7]

The tactics of terror have never been restricted to any particular social stratum; or at least, defining the appropriate class labels to everyone's satisfaction is an impossible task. "Working class" in San Salvador is a very different status from "working class" in San Francisco. The socialist teacher will claim to be working class, of course; yet in the eyes of an unskilled laborer he or she will most definitely appear as middle class. In the absence of constant parameters, such labels can be said only to imply an attitude, a state of mind. This is confirmed by incidents of terror campaigns embarked upon by self-appointed representatives of some "oppressed" sector of the community who throughout the campaign are unable to identify with, or relate to the actions of those they are setting out to save.

The revolutionary terrorist will blame this failure to gain mass support on apathy. He will explain that this is one of the reasons that terrorist methods are employed instead of the often protracted techniques of peaceful persuasion. In the absence of a convincing "why," the terrorist emphasizes with alarming enthusiasm the "how."

Regardless of proclaimed class, research and statistics

indicate that a high percentage of terrorists have been and are more what we would call middle class or even above. Ulrike Meinhof of Baader-Meinhof infamy was the daughter of wealthy art historians, although she was brought up by a nonparent, also an art historian.[8] Ilich Ramirez Sanches, also known as "the Jackal" or "Carlos"—arguably the best known of international terrorists and leader of the group which seized members of the OPEC conference in Vienna in 1975—is the son of a millionaire lawyer.[9] Giangiacomo Feltrinelli, Italian left-wing activist and sponsor of several terrorist actions, was a multimillionaire publisher.[10]

The search for the pigeon-holeable terrorist is ongoing. While it is possible to isolate certain characteristics of individuals or groups and thereby show that there is some common denominator, one would have to be very bold indeed to claim that he had identified a pattern of characteristics accurate for all terrorists.

In an effort to assemble data that would be of use in a terrorist-versus-government confrontation, the Italian secret service commissioned Professor Franco Ferracuti of Rome to examine and collate information on several thousand known terrorists. The authorities hoped to be able to predict the probable behavior of terrorists from different groups in negotiation scenarios. Would terrorists bargain reasonably and calmly or fly into a murderous rage and kill indiscriminately if their demands were not met without hesitation?

To this end, the known sociological backgrounds of convicted terrorists and those awaiting trial were compared, and the terrorists themselves subjected to psychological testing. The results, in essence, were that both left- and right-wing groups contained some people whose childhood had been disrupted in some way (by absentee fathers, for example). Left-wing terrorists, according to the data produced, were more likely to have successfully completed their educations. Many of the leftist individuals concerned had found a career niche. A higher percentage of those from the extreme right were found to have had broken educations. The predominant social background was middle/lower-middle class.

A higher percentage of women were found in the leftist groups than among the rightist ones, and their value to the cause was rated more highly among the leftist males. Many right-wing terrorists implied that the presence of women in their groups was tolerated rather than encouraged. Drug users were not found in any significant numbers in the left-wing groups, while those of the right contained a far higher proportion. The right-wing groups also contained a higher percentage of people who were defined by Professor Ferracuti as having "not entirely normal" behavior characteristics.[11]

No analysis of the term "not entirely normal" behavior as it was employed in this context was given. In the absence of any specific definition, I am inclined to interpret the term as simply meaning behavior that is significantly different from that considered by the majority to be normal. It was emphasized by Professor Ferracuti that the abnormality referred to did not amount to insanity.[12]

While this Italian study of the sociological backgrounds and psychological profiles of Italian terrorists identified differences between left-wing terrorists and those from the neo-Fascist right, attempts in other geographical areas to determine qualities which lend themselves to general application have provided varying results. A recent Turkish survey, for example, found that there existed no significant differences in sociological backgrounds between terrorists from the extreme left-wing and extreme right-wing groups operating in that country. This is worthy of note if only because the members of such groups have been killing one another for decades.

During this survey, Turkish psychologists observed that, compared to a control group, the terrorists had significantly lower intelligence quotients. Also, it was found that terrorists who had killed had similar personality profiles to non-terrorist, criminal killers.

It is safe to say that the nationalist/separatist groups of today contain a higher percentage of individuals from a low economic background than do the left-wing groups. The IRA and INLA (Irish National Liberation Army) are good examples of this, although they are supported to some extent by a political cadre comprised mainly of well-educated, middle-class/intellectual/white-collar types. This is also true of the Basque ETA.

It is to be expected that these groups–as distinct from the purely political ones–should be thus comprised, as those elements of the society which are content with "foreign" control or domination are most likely to be in advantageous positions enjoying a comfortable and pleasant lifestyle. It is the nature of things that those people not able to exploit or take advantage of a given situation will seek to blame their lot on an authority they see as alien.

NOTES

1. Walter Laqueur, *Terrorism* (London: Weidenfield and Nicolson, 1977), p. 121.
2. J. Bowyer Bell, *A Time of Terror* (New York: Basic Books, 1978), p. 7.
3. *London Observer* newspaper team, *Siege* (London: The Observer, 1980), p. 89.
4. *London Times,* 24 November 1985.
5. Walter Laqueur, p. 120.
6. Ibid., p. 121.
7. *London Times,* November 1985.
8. Walter Laqueur, p. 207.
9. A 1975 police photo of "Carlos"–looking every bit the innocent–is to be found in Charles Freeman, *Terrorism* (London: Batsford Academic and Educa-

tional, 1981), p. 33.

10. Walter Laqueur, p. 211.

11. From the British television documentary "Terrorism," shown nationally in 1985, in which Franco Ferracuti was interviewed about his findings.

12. From the same program.

4

Training

The training of a terrorist effectively begins with his introduction to the cause he will work for, and this may conceivably occur during childhood. Indeed, terrorist traditions are impressed upon young community members in many parts of the world where a historical injustice or nationalist/separatist issue remains unresolved. Ireland, the Middle East, and Armenia are but three examples.

Extremist political ideologies are also promulgated openly by many individuals whose motives are questionable to say the least. There is little doubt, for instance, that many of the Western world's educational facilities have been "infiltrated" by proponents of some extremist political ideology simply with a view to disseminating agitative views and doctrines. Teachers, lecturers, professors–whom one would expect to present a fairly balanced, objective view of world events, political doctrines, and techniques for changing a system with which one does not agree–frequently appear to be so fervently committed to the left-wing of the political spectrum that only the most mature and experienced students in their charge could hope to resist what often amounts to pressure to adopt similar, leftist philosophies. The fact that adoption of such philosophies by large numbers of people, or the introduction of a political system based upon such philosophies, would inevitably lead to partial or total removal of the freedom which permits the current instructors to disseminate their views seems often to go unnoticed, or, at the least, unmentioned. Thus one is forced to ask what the real, ultimate objectives of these people are.

My own opinion is that, in the West at least, the actual objective is nothing more than destabilization of the existing regimes. I doubt that serious thought is given to *exactly* what type of system would be introduced should this destabilization result in the incumbent's downfall. Examples of Marxist teaching staff using their positions to actively engage in propaganda dissemination, recruitment, and even assault campaigns are not hard to find. The London *Daily Mail* newspaper, December 9, 1981, carried an article about John Penny, a lecturer in sociology at Mid-Cheshire College of Further Education. He had been jailed for fifteen months for recruiting and controlling a hit-team of left-wing activists to attack the National Front (an extreme right-wing group that is violently racist). A member of the Socialist Workers Party of England, he had previously been convicted for disorderly conduct while picketing during a strike. He had kept this conviction a secret from the college authorities.

At the time of writing, and against the backdrop of what would seem to be a right-wing revival among American college and university students, the extreme left-wing groups in England are intensifying their efforts to indoctrinate the young and malleable mind. CND (Campaign for Nuclear Disarmament) badges are displayed by teachers on vehicles and on clothes, and CND membership forms are offered to pupils. This is occurring in schools attended by children, many of whom are less than twelve years old and obviously too young to analyze the implications of such material independently of the biased propaganda being aimed at them.

Extreme left-wing and right-wing racist literature is frequently distributed in British schools–some by "outsiders," some by members of the teaching staff itself. In much the same way that children in Soviet-influenced parts of Central America and Africa are taught to count with reference to such everyday items as rifle magazines and bullets, the political influence has found its way into junior-school mathematics in England in the form of questions which require the pupil to calculate the percentage differences between white workers and black workers in South Africa.

It is also interesting to note, that while the Soviet International Department has offered to send, free, to British schools and colleges Russian books extolling the benefits of the Soviet System and denouncing the evils of Western capitalism, comparable works detailing the democratic systems are banned from Russia.

A degree of what might be called "pre-training conditioning," then, is likely to influence an individual's decision regarding whether or not some cause is worth supporting actively and, if so, what methods he thinks are justified in employing toward furthering those beliefs. The reaction to any stimulus will, of course, be tempered or heightened by the existing psychological state of the individual. Assuming that strong moral convictions or mental aberrations cause an individual to opt for the terrorist approach, the next logical step is for him to seek practical training in the required skills.

In the case of a lone wolf, inspired perhaps by the deeds of others before him or frustrated beyond despair into ill-considered action, training may simply take the form of reading the "right" books. However, the techniques that have been used in the past to effect a given result are often too numerous to permit an easy choice, or perhaps not quite appropriate. The determined newcomer may, of necessity, have to develop his own techniques.

Credit for ingenuity and initiative should not be denied those without access to existing source material; however, there is available a wealth of published information for the aspiring terrorist. Most of it can be purchased readily and legally. *The Anarchist's Cookbook* by William Powell is one such book. It was the inspiration for the explosive device that Zvonko Busic—as one of the members of the Fighters for Free Croatia group—used to kill bomb-disposal officer Brian Murray as he and his colleagues from the New York bomb squad worked to disarm it at Rodman Neck in September 1976.[1]

Busic had planted the bomb in a New York subway station locker as a means of indicating to the authorities that his threats should be taken seriously. Busic's other "explosive devices," which he used to hijack TWA Flight 355 on September 10, 1976, were nothing more than assemblages of scrap wire and clay.

Books such as Powell's detail the construction and use of weapons ranging from the Molotov cocktail (gasoline bomb) to high explosives made from materials as apparently innocent as sugar and ammonium nitrate fertilizer. Techniques needed to make these explosives, as well as the nail bomb, the pipe bomb, and the tin-can grenade—three other favorites of urban terrorists—are among the first to be learned by the would-be terrorist.

Many terror groups have prepared training manuals with a view both to disseminating practical information and establishing a group identity. Like most other aspects of the terrorist field, manuals are not new. Detailed, sophisticated manuals on mayhem were in circulation a hundred years or more before the ideas of Castro and Mao were similarly documented. Descriptions of the fundamental Communist guerrilla technique of gradually amalgamating successful guerrilla units into a conventional army were also proferred by various anarchist commentators in the early nineteenth century.

In World War II, Britain's SOE (Special Operations Executive) produced literally tens of thousands of copies of a thirty-two page booklet detailing the principles of sabotage and behind-the-lines fighting. These were dropped to resistance groups in occupied Europe. Here the motive was not only to teach but also to inculcate a feeling of "belonging" among the fighters.

An Argentinian terror group, the "Montoneros"—active in the 1970s and able to list among their "victories" the kidnap and murder of ex-President Aramburu—created "Regulations for Organizing Political Military Activity" and "Military Instruction Manual." We have already mentioned Marighella's *Minimanual.* Perhaps the most interesting of terrorist training manuals are those produced by the Italian Red Brigade. In "Security Rules and Work Methods," Red Brigade operatives are shown how important it is for the urban guerrilla to create an impression of respectability. It recommends that apartments always be kept clean, tidy, and properly furnished. The outside of the property in use by operatives is to be a picture of domestic normality—with nameplate, entrance light, etc. A window box is suggested as being another positive image component. When selecting a property to rent, the operative is warned to choose one in which the landlord is not resident and which is located in such an area as to make covert surveillance by police and other agencies difficult or impossible. Readers of the manual are encouraged to fit strong locks to doors and windows, to spend time washing their car, to tend any garden areas, and otherwise to maintain the required air of innocence.

When an individual has decided to support some existing terrorist movement, he usually has little difficulty in establishing initial contact. By far the majority of extremist/terrorist groups these days operate a political or public-relations wing, the primary purpose of which is to disseminate information pertaining to the cause in such a manner as to elicit public sympathy, and, where possible, to raise funds. These wings usually deny any knowledge of the terrorist activity perpetrated in the name of the same cause, and, if it seems prudent, even denounce the perpetrators outright. With very few exceptions, the would-be terrorist is not welcomed with open arms, handed a weapon, and sent into active duty. Infiltration is the constant concern of terror groups, and any unknown newcomer will be required to undergo a period of probation and assessment.

The cornerstone of any training scheme is political indoctrination. This applies to the nationalist/separatist groups as well as to the revolutionary type. This "political re-education," however, may often be little more than learning the required rhetoric. In the early stages of engagement with a group operating in an urban environment, much of the volunteer's work consists of agitation and disruption. Thus initial training comprises in part learning techniques directed toward destabilization of the established order while remaining (just) within the bounds of the law. Crowd incitement, propaganda dissemination, industrial-dispute provocation, strike leadership, and media manipulation will be included in most training courses. In Great Britain, the Workers Revolutionary Party owns various training centers, the most notorious being a large country property in Derbyshire. Literally thousands of industrial activists have "passed out" from this establishment during the past few years,[2] all of them expert in turning a minor dispute into a massive worker/employer/government confrontation.

The British Communist party regularly sends selected groups for overseas training sessions, and the International Marxist Group and a variety of other left-wing associations provide training in most forms of "soft" activism. The larger of these groups actively recruit from within schools and universities through leaflet campaigns and through the large numbers of teachers/professors who subscribe to their views.

Small, newly formed groups without contacts in the established terror organizations now have the opportunity to learn a variety of skills in privately operated training camps. Such camps are growing in number, both in the United States and Europe, and are often to be found advertised in specialist magazines catering to the military and gun enthusiast. The operators of such camps claim to be able to teach trainees everything from escape, evasion, and survival skills to the use of weapons and explosives. The quality of training provided and the degree of selectivity exercised toward applicants vary considerably from camp to camp. Some camps are, by all accounts, little more than attempts to cash in on the current wave of militarism; others are more serious and are staffed by known and respected professionals.

Many of these camps are unable to produce highly qualified personnel. Individuals hoping to establish themselves as free-lance soldier types will discover to their cost—and probably the cost of those serving with them—that a weekend course in most anything leaves out as much as it covers. From the terrorist point of view, however, such brief training sessions may be more than satisfactory. The potential enemy is likely to be unarmed and not expecting an attack. Under these circumstances simply knowing how to remove a safety catch or attach a detonator may be enough. Also, a terrorist group may be primarily concerned with vehicle-based actions (such as abductions). Many of these camps offer a defensive-driving course—a good opportunity for the group to study such techniques and work out possible ways to defeat them. Similarly, by claiming in these camps to require instruction in "rescue actions" of the type a mercenary might have to carry out, a terrorist group or individual might learn a great deal that would help them to execute a kidnapping or many another terrorist action.

A more disturbing aspect of the training-camp phenomenon is that a certain number of such facilities are provided by governments keen to encourage the terrorist cause. "Carlos," the Venezuelan contract terrorist—educated, incidentally, in Moscow[3]—attended training camps in Palestine. Elements of the Baader-Meinhof group are known to have received advanced training in Jordan alongside Palestinian terrorists.[4] Indeed, the Middle East has come to be regarded in many circles as one large training center for terrorists and extremists of various persuasions.

The Ayatollah Khomeini's regime in Iran continues to support terrorist movements, and training in a variety of weapons is available to those he considers to be furthering the fight against his declared religious and political enemies. Col. Muammar Khadafi in Libya has trained and equipped terrorist groups from as far afield as Germany and Ireland. The standard of training available through these and other governments, such as that of Syria, is high. It is on a professional military level.

Khadafi's every move is, of course, now closely monitored by Western security agencies and, consequently, he has of late backed off somewhat with regard to his overt recruitment of foreign terrorist operatives. Nevertheless, Libya maintains several terrorist training camps within her borders. At the time of writing, a typical pay scale for recruits passing through such a camp is about one-thousand dollars per month for non-African and non-Arab personnel, and approximately four-hundred dollars per month for personnel from the Arab and African states. These fees are paid in addition to housing and food allocations. One proviso, however, is that upon "graduation," the newly trained terrorists are permitted to take only 50 percent of their accumulated earnings out of the country.

The would-be terrorist, then, should he find himself in the "right" place at the "right" time, may be presented with an opportunity to earn considerable sums of money. The only requirement—aside, perhaps, from a degree of military expertise or aptitude—is that the individual be prepared to serve one of this century's most unstable and dangerous dictators. To some, an ability to thus serve comes easily. Former CIA operative Frank Terpil has sold both expertise and materiel to Colonel Khadafi since the mid-1970s. His attitude seems to typify that of many "gun for hire" terrorists and terrorist regime supporters whose actions are very likely to result in the death of their own kind, that is, nationals of their own country. This attitude, which implies a peculiar sort of rationale on the part of the operative, is best summed up in Terpil's own words, spoken in response to a request by "revolutionaries" for weapons and poisons: "If you're knocking off Americans, it'll cost you 40 percent more."

Terrorist training sponsored by Syria, Iran, and Libya is known to include conventional guerrilla tactics and weaponry as well as specialist techniques–suicide assaults, anti-rescue techniques for aircraft hijacking, etc. Mock-ups of aircraft are used during such training so that terrorists can learn where a rescue assault team is most likely to try to enter. The terrorists are able to learn in a realistic situation such strategies as positioning passengers in either the most vulnerable parts of the aircraft–so that an assault by rescuers will almost certainly result in hostage deaths–or the most inaccessible areas–so that the rescuers are forced to fight a pitched battle before they can reach them. The terrorists are also taught how to booby-trap aircraft to forestall rescue attempts. Media manipulation is also emphasized where applicable, and hijack-team personnel are instructed not to execute any publicity-valuable action until the world media are present. Where exploitation of normal publicity media is not practical–as in a suicide attack–the training instructs that the group itself be provided with video equipment with which to record the event. Footage may then be distributed later. Recently released video recordings of suicide attacks perpetrated by PLO elements against the Israeli military in the Middle East have included interviews with the perpetrators in which they explained the motive and justification for the attack. The emotional value–and therefore the publicity/propaganda value–of such techniques is very high indeed.

The willingness of certain regimes to sponsor terrorism shows that there are links of cooperation between terrorist groups. These links will continue, however, only so long as each organization's acts further the aims of another group or at least do not impede them.

Even in Northern Ireland where one might expect the psychological equivalents of barbed wire and concrete barriers to permanently obstruct the techniques of cooperation between Catholic and Protestant terror groups, the realization that an occasional and temporary coalition—albeit one born of necessity—can be mutually beneficial has dawned on many. To this end, meetings are now held in a public house on the Shankhill Road, Belfast, between representatives of the Irish National Liberation Army (INLA) and the Protestant Ulster Defence Association (UDA). These groups are among the most violent of those operating at each extreme of the Irish religious/political spectrum. Other factions attend such meetings as well, factions which are designed to establish areas of operation for each group without the need to resort to (oftentimes) self-destructive territorial warfare. Such meetings also facilitate the planning of certain robberies (generally those likely to net a very high return) and fencing operations (the sale and distribution of stolen goods). This cooperation does not amount to joint operation in the traditional sense, but rather enables a mutually agreeable, mutually profitable strategy to be worked out with regard to some specific project.

The IRA, for example, might arrange with elements of the UDA to rob a bank in UDA-controlled territory. In return for a promise of non-intervention and no revenge on the part of the UDA, the IRA will allow them to launder the stolen funds through their business fronts—for a percentage, of course. Similarly, a UDA group might need intelligence about the impending activities of the security forces in a certain part of the city. They will "buy" this information from the IRA group in return for some service which the Catholic group is unable to provide for itself. The UDA operates a number of legitimate security companies in various parts of Belfast (Leader Enterprises, based in East Belfast, is one such company). It is not unheard of for this

Protestant organization to be employed by an IRA group to guard a Catholic construction site. The IRA takes a cut of the profits, and everybody is happy!

Many groups will accept support and training from regimes whose long-term aims are, in fact, opposed to their own. This points up a fundamental aspect of the type of extremist doctrines found among terrorist organizations: Groups which have helped achieve an end may be destroyed if they have helped for the wrong reasons or if their continuance becomes a hindrance to new goals. Of course, until the emergence of such an overt conflict, each group or regime involved believes it is using the other. Ultimately, the most powerful or ruthless will survive.

As the majority of training areas—private and state-run—are known to the security forces of various countries, the opportunity for intelligence-gathering by surveillance of individuals traveling to and from these areas is not wasted. Such surveillance, together with effective immigration-control techniques, can prevent a terrorist or group of terrorists from entering a country with a view to perpetrating some terrorist action. Sensible screening of this sort can keep terrorist operations within manageable parameters. For example, a young, unmarried traveler with a one-way ticket purchased for cash, whose reason for the visit is "tourism" and whose passport shows that he has recently visited an area controlled by regimes which are unfriendly to the country he is now seeking to enter, is likely to present a greater risk than a family group, traveling with small children and paying by American Express. Such groups of people can be excluded from a surveillance project. Of course there can be no guarantee that the old woman in a wheelchair is not actually a terrorist sympathizer intent on the massacre of her fellow travelers. Nevertheless, practicality requires that surveillance be limited to high-risk categories; and experience has generally shown this approach to be effective.

The widespread availability of convenient passports—

forged, obtained legally using deception, or provided by terrorist-sympathizing regimes—makes it difficult on occasion to determine what category of risk a traveler should be placed in. We have seen that a warning bell may be sounded if a passport shows recent travels to countries in which terrorist training centers exist, or in which terrorist activity is known to be encouraged. But if the individual has obtained a "clean" passport, this indicator will be missing.[5] In an effort to overcome such problems, we may see in the future the use of psychological screening tests or stress analysis tests at ports of entry. VSA (Voice Stress Analyzer) equipment is used by some police departments and even some journalists with a view to detecting stress in an interviewee's voice that might indicate deception. Such devices are far from infallible, but as an indicator or as a deterrent they may prove useful. In the latter context, their use, for example, at air terminals, would be well publicized.

Travel by individuals on certain dates can also be used to assess threat potential. Assuming that a traveler fits into some other "possible risk" category, as determined by the prevailing trends, further suspicion will be aroused if the date of travel coincides with or implies a connection with some event known or calculated to be of significance to a terrorist group. This event might typically be the anniversary of the death of a martyr, of the annexing of some territory, of the earlier arrest of activists, of the assassination of a terrorist group leader by opposition elements; or the visit to the place in question of, for example, a minister of a country with policies or views contrary to those of a given terrorist group, and so on.

The British police and security services regularly monitor the movements of members of the Irish community who travel from England to Ireland to attend IRA parades and celebrations. Once individuals are identified as IRA sympathizers, their friends and acquaintances are also placed under surveillance. These techniques were instrumental in bringing to justice many of the perpetrators of mainland bombings during the IRA campaign in 1974. This series of attacks culminated in bombings of two Birmingham public houses, The Mulberry Bush and The Tavern In The Town, for which no warnings were issued and in which twenty-one people were killed and 162 injured.[6]

A SELECTION OF TERRORIST TRAINING CAMP LOCATIONS

Many of the terrorist training camps in the following list are effectively military academies. Individuals who successfully complete a certain course receive a graduation certificate/certificate of proficiency. Al Fatah members have also graduated from the military academy proper in Havana, Cuba. This dual use of an establishment intended initially for less controversial use is quite common. The Soviet Union created a sabotage-training school in Prague, Czechoslovakia, specifically for the training of terrorist operatives, in this instance Palestinian nationalists. The course was taught by Soviet and East German trainers and lasted about six weeks. After graduating from this course, the participants were transferred on to another, four-month training program at Kosiče in Slovakia.

Other camps known to be used by international terror groups exist in:

1. Baku, Crimea
2. Tashkent, Crimea
3. Odessa, Crimea
4. Sinferopol, Crimea
5. Karlovy Vary, Czechoslovakia
6. Ostrova, Czechoslovakia
7. Doupov, Czechoslovakia
8. Lake Balaton, Hungary
9. Varna, Bulgaria
10. Pankov, East Germany
11. Finsterwald, East Germany
12. Nahar El Barad, Tripoli, Libya

13. Tocra, Libya
14. Hit, Iraq
15. Baghdad, Iraw
16. Tarhuma, Libya
17. Misurate, Libya
18. Sirte, Libya

This is but a partial list of camps. Sites used for the training of terrorists also exist in Iran, Lebanon, North Korea, South Yemen, Eire, Algeria, and elsewhere.

NOTES

1. J. Bowyer Bell, *A Time of Terror* (New York: Basic Books, 1978), p. 13.

2. Ian Will, *The Big Brother Society* (London: Harrap, 1983), p. 109.

3. "Carlos"–Ilich Ramirez Sanchez–received much of his Soviet-sponsored training at the Patrice Lumumba Friendship University in Moscow. This establishment was founded in 1960 by Khruschev and has been KGB dominated from the onset. Its purpose is to indoctrinate foreign students in the skills of subversion and revolution. See Chapman Pincher, *The Secret Offensive* (London: Sidgwick and Jackson, 1985), p. 245. Also Mike Hoare, *Mercenary,* Corgi paperback ed. (London: Transworld, 1978), pp. 287–294.

4. Christopher Dobson and Ronald Payne, *The Weapons of Terror* (London: Macmillan, 1979), p. 154.

5. Reports from Rome in October 1985, following the arrest and interrogation of Shi'ite Muslim terrorists, stated that some four hundred passports were available to other terrorist operatives, many of whom were planning suicide attacks. Few of such passports are "fake"; rather, they are taken from real citizens or "doubled" by terrorist-sympathetic states. To *double* a passport is to issue a second copy of an already issued passport to

some other person.

6. Brian Gibson, *The Birmingham Bombs* (London: Barry Rose, 1976), p. 135.

5

Financial Support

In times past, many an aspiring terrorist group could exist and operate without the need for external financial support, and very often campaigns would be funded entirely by one or more of the group's enthusiastic members. If specific aims (assuming there were any, for such was not always the case) had not been achieved by the time this source dried up, however, the group would face two alternatives: cease operations or turn to robbery, extortion, or blackmail. It was this latter course that was most often adopted. Sometimes, of course, a wealthy sponsor would befriend a group and, while taking no active part in campaigns, would maintain a supply of cash. The Irish Revolutionary Brotherhood, a nineteenth-century organization—founded, incidentally, with a four-hundred-dollar donation from well-wishers in the United States[1]—was helped in no small measure by a famous billiards champion of the time. And the Spanish anarchist Francisco Ferrer was given a million francs by a French lady friend.[2]

A decision to turn to robbery was not always made lightly, and more than one group was to split up because of ethical conflicts among members. In the early 1900s terrorists fighting for the independence of India expended much effort in selecting the most acceptable way to secure funds by robbery. Some wanted to target only government funds, others; believed that money should also be taken from those who had obtained it by dishonest means. It was even suggested that records be kept of the amounts and individuals concerned, so that repayment could be made once independence was secured.[3]

Several terrorists have commented that too much money available to a group has a decidedly negative effect, usually beginning with the purchase of unnecessary items, items related to personal want as opposed to need.[4] Philosophies of austerity within terrorist groups are frequently enforced with a ruthless literalness. This is illustrated by an incident which occurred in the spring of 1972 in Karuizawa, Japan, in which fourteen members of the United Red Army were tortured and killed by their comrades for "crimes" which, in the case of four females thus murdered, included wearing make-up and showing affection for the opposite sex.[5]

"Promaterialism" splinter elements often find that their new "capitalist" status brings with it danger of attack from their former comrades. Suheir Muhsin, one-time commander of the PLO group Saika, was killed in his luxurious retreat on the French Riviera by young PLO fighters disgusted with the extravagant lifestyle of their leaders.[6] In this latter case, at least the "wealth" is real and considerable. Yasser Arafat's PLO is estimated to have assets in the region of six billion dollars. In many Arab countries the PLO maintains its own health-care service. Arafat's brother, Fathi, is the head of the Palestinian Red Crescent, an Islamic equivalent of the Western Red Cross; according to Israeli sources, Arafat's aide, Abu Abbas, is paid one hundred thousand dollars a month.[7] This bears comparison to groups that split from Arafat who are hard-pressed to find spare funds for weapons.

At a summit in Baghdad in 1978, the Arabs decided to donate three hundred million dollars a year to the PLO for the period 1979 to 1989 as the "official" political representative of the Palestinian people. The majority of payments are made by the oil-producing nations. Estimates for 1985 of funds thus raised by the PLO are: from Saudi Arabia, 85.7 million dollars;

Kuwait, 47.1 million dollars; Iraq, 44 million dollars; 34.3 million dollars from the United Arab Emirates; 47 million from Libya; 19.8 million from Qatar, and 21.4 million from Algeria. There is also a voluntary payment asked of all Palestinians living abroad. It is worth noting that some of the contributing nations–Libya especially–often fail to supply their full part of the payment. In the *London Times* newspaper article in December 1985, it was reported that one of Yasser Arafat's senior aides, Abo Iyad, was complaining: "Khadafi has blown too much money in Uganda and Chad to have any left for his Palestinian brethren."[8]

It would be unfair to exclude the Soviets from any discourse on terrorist funds. The Soviets have always supported terrorism in the West, since any disruption and destabilization thus caused can only be to their benefit. It matters not precisely what the aims of a particular group may be, and it is a mistake to imagine that Soviet money only finds its way into Communist revolutionary coffers. Providing a group is opposed to the incumbent regime of a country, and providing that the Kremlin would like to see that same regime undermined or destroyed, the group can count on Soviet aid.

Via the International Department and the KGB *Komitet Gosudarstvennoi Bezopasnosti,* or State Security Committee), the Politburo has helped such diverse terror groups as ZAPU (Zimbabwe Africa Peoples Union), the Egyptian Fundamentalists, the PLO, the IRA, and the Baader-Meinhof group. In the 1960s a terror group known as the Weathermen perpetrated various bombings in the United States and, through infiltrated agitators, frequently provoked street fighting between anti-Vietnam War protesters and the police. Members of this group, with the help of Cubans, were also responsible for bomb incidents in Quebec in support of French Canadian separatists (although their real intent was simply the destruction of the democratic system). In June 1982, a former member of the Weathermen group, Larry Grathwohl, appeared on Canadian television and explained, among other things, how, using Soviet money, the Cuban intelligence service recruited Weathermen operatives from among radical young Americans visiting Havana and trained them in bombing techniques. On the same program, a former Cuban intelligence officer stated that the Soviets were behind the whole Weathermen/ Cuban involvement.[9]

More innovative techniques may also be used by terrorist and extremist groups both to solicit funds and to spread their version of the truth regarding various "injustices." On sale at the time of writing in several Western countries is a record by Robert Wyatt and the SWAPO singers. SWAPO actually stands for the South West African People's Organization and, according to the information supplied with the record, is: "the national liberation movement of Namibia which has been fighting since 1960 for the independence of Namibia, illegally occupied at present by South Africa. 70,000 Namibians have been forced into exile by the brutal South African repression. . . . They have fled the most intense military occupation in the world today. . . . Innocent civilians are killed at random, tortured in detention centers or disappear almost every day."[10]

SWAPO might alternatively be described as a terrorist organization which seeks to take control in South West Africa, and in fact its tactics to date invalidate any claims to the contrary. The (mis)information supplied with this musical offering, headlined, "All proceeds to SWAPO," fails to mention at all the fact that FAPLA (Army of the Popular Front for the Liberation of Angola), the Soviet-trained army of Angola, gives arms and other aid to SWAPO, and that its "fight for independence" includes killing politicians, village headmen, and shopkeepers; the laying of mines and sabotage; and the abduction of civilian "recruits." The group's aims are in reality the construction of a Marxist style regime; "a classless society, free from exploitation, based on the ideals of scientific socialism."[11]

For the terrorist group advocating a nationalist/separatist policy and operating from a base or bases in or close to its area of operations, there exists the opportunity to establish legitimate business enterprises with a view to earning and laundering funds. In Northern Ireland, for example, the IRA effectively controls the local taxi services. Cab drivers are required to pay a "voluntary" donation to the revolutionary cause in order that "their safety can be guaranteed." Vehicle hijack is rife in the area, and only when word is spread that such-and-such a cab should be left alone can the driver feel fairly sure he will not be first on the list of possible targets. In reality, the insurance is not so much that the driver will *not* be harmed or have his vehicle appropriated if he contributes, but rather that this will be an inevitable consequence of his failure to do so. Some drivers are pro-IRA in any case and willingly perform various transport and intelligence-gathering services for the group.[12]

Indeed, in parts of Belfast, it is the paramilitary terrorist groups themselves that actually own and operate the main taxi services. People's Taxis and Falls Taxis are two IRA-sponsored examples. The legal front for these operations is known as The Taxi Drivers Association. Drivers pay this association some fifty dollars per week in what one could describe as membership fees and an additional eight hundred dollars per year (approximately) for insurance. By and large, the drivers will always purchase their fuel from Provisional IRA (PIRA) controlled garages, and have repairs carried out at the same places. For several years, no buses operated in Catholic Belfast–PIRA saw to that–but of late, improved security force measures have enabled the return of a bus service of sorts. Threats by PIRA against "freelance" taxi operators are common. In September 1986, the terrorist group again announced that unless taxi operators not sympathetic to the cause publicly declared that they would not accept security force personnel as passengers any more, they would be "executed."

Not to be outdone, Protestant terrorist groups have also established their taxi service. Operating primarily in the Shankhill Road area of Belfast, it is estimated that the Ulster Volunteer Force (UVF) controls approximately one hundred taxis. The legitimate front for this project is the North Belfast Mutual Association. Drivers pay this organization about five dollars per week for various services and are offered a reduction in their annual insurance premiums if they undertake to buy all their fuel from Association-controlled outlets. It has been claimed that a further weekly payment of about fifty dollars (a donation to the UVF in all but name) is demanded from drivers. It is also believed that, like the PIRA-operated taxis, the UVF-organized taxi drivers collect protection money and perform other services which further the Protestant cause.

Gaming machines are another method by which funds can be raised by groups who have access to high-density urban areas. Such machines can be installed—legally in many cases—with the cooperation of a sympathetic club owner or an unsympathetic one who is in little doubt what fate will befall him and the club should he decline the offer of additional machines! While one might consider the potential rewards from such sources to be minimal, this is not the case. A British police estimate of the amount one well-sited gaming machine can make in a year is forty-five thousand dollars. Imagine, then, the profit from a dozen such machines in even one busy Belfast bar.

NOTES

1. Walter Laqueur, *Terrorism* (London: Weidenfield and Nicolson, 1977), p. 87.

2. Ibid., p. 87.

3. Ibid., p. 87.

4. Reading several of the available works on terrorists and their philosophies will confirm this.

5. Gerald McKnight, *The Mind of the Terrorist* (London: Michael Joseph, 1974), pp. index: U.R.A. (United Red Army).

6. *London Times,* 9 December 1985.

7. Ibid.

8. Ibid.

9. This confirmed evidence was given by FBI agents in November 1981.

10. This project's European base has a post office box number in London: P.O. Box 16, London NW5 2LW. It appears to be organized by the Namibia Support Committee, which also convenes the Campaign against the Namibian Uranium Contracts, SWAPO Women's Solidarity Campaign, Repression and Political Prisoners Campaign, and the Health Collective and Action on Namibia Publications.

11. From a quote in the West German news weekly *Der Spiegel,* 1978, of a SWAPO party leader, Sam Nujoma. Reprinted in *Soldier of Fortune,* February 1984. This issue of *Soldier of Fortune* gives a broad overview of SWAPO's policies and techniques, and describes the measures used by SADF (South African Defence Force) to combat them.

12. Various sources, including conversations with British soldiers and IRA sympathizers.

6

Strategies

THE STEPPING STONE STRATEGY

When a terrorist group is frustrated in striking at what it considers its legitimate targets, it must find a means of effective actions at a point of lesser resistance. Thus emerges what might be called the stepping stone strategy. For example, the aim to seize or kill some specific individual, who, in his own country, is beyond the reach of the terrorists, often provokes the move of attacking that individual when he is visiting another country. Visiting diplomats frequently go without the high levels of protection they receive in their own countries when they go to meet with foreign counterparts. Protection will be given by the host government, of course, but this is often less effective, particularly in a country where terrorist activity is less frequent. The victim may also be on a holiday trip or some other personal errand where high-level security measures would be awkward. Thus the target is more vulnerable than at home, and a successful attack may be carried out. But this is only the first advantage of the attack in a neutral country.

The stepping stone strategy is in essence a deliberate attempt by the terrorists to legitimize further targets. How this works can be seen from the following example. Armenian terrorists killed Colonel Attila Altikat, a Turkish military attaché, in Canada.[1] This provoked, as could be expected, an intense security effort on the part of the Canadian authorities. Some of those responsible for the murder were arrested and imprisoned. The Armenian terrorists were then able to claim that the Canadian government was holding "political" prisoners. Thus *all* Canadian interests now became "legitimate" targets for the Armenian terrorist group.

PSYCHOLOGICAL OPERATIONS

Psychological Operations (PsyOps) can be broadly defined as any operation calculated to influence the thoughts and thereby the actions of a target through the application of persuasive measures. The applicable techniques may be used by and against terrorist organizations. Indeed, much of the antiterrorist activity enacted on our behalf by the intelligence agencies take this form. This is to be expected, of course, as the majority of seriously damaging terrorist actions perpetrated against the West are defined by a major terrorist sponsor–the Soviet Union–as "active measures" *(aktivnyye merpriyatiya)*. These "active measures" include all aspects of the undeclared war that the Soviets–directly or via their satellite regimes–constantly wage against the West in an effort to fulfill Stalin's original plans for "asserting the further power of the Soviets." But "active measures" almost equates, in essence, to PsyOps.

Both terms cover acts of selective assassination and isolated incidents of violence. Thus terrorism itself might be thought of as an extreme example of psychological warfare, since the basic tactic of all terrorism is the inculcation of fear, confusion, and uncertainty, rather than pure force of arms. In the typical scenario, a psychological-operations/active-measures target–which might be a group, institution, or individual–will be affected in such a manner as to create the illusion that the effect generated is spontaneous or the result of some uncoordinated sequence of events. In this fashion the target may remain oblivious to the fact that his reaction has been manipulated deliberately in furthering the interests of the instigators.

The "peace movement" in Europe, for example, is being used as a vehicle by the Soviets to try to decouple the United States and the rest of NATO. While many of the movement's members are well aware of this, some prefer not to accept the truth, or consider it somehow "incidental" to the removal of nuclear weapons.

One of the main Soviet agencies for conducting anti-Western active measures is the International Department. This department is the modern-day "Comintern," Lenin's subversive organization established initially to promote Soviet-type revolutions in foreign countries. The International Department is currently headed by Boris Ponomarev, an eighty-year-old who has held the position for some thirty years. The department is staffed by several hundred officers, some of whom are stationed abroad in embassies. Its role includes control of all the Communist front groups operating under various covers in target countries, their funding, and guidance under the changing party line. It also maintains links with foreign Communist regimes and attempts to keep its actions beneficial to Moscow. It controls agent-provocateurs in target areas, oversees the operation of clandestine radio stations, arranges disinformation projects, plants forgeries calculated to destabilize the targeted regimes, organizations, and their supports, and along with other departments, "national liberation" movements and certain international terrorist groups. According to intelligence analysts Richard Shultz and Roy Godson, some ten to fifteen thousand people are employed full time on Soviet active measures.

The distribution of agitative propaganda material among co-workers by employees of some company or organization supportive of an extremist political movement or nationalist/separatist group likewise falls under the PsyOps heading.

There has traditionally been little private sector PsyOp activity from the right-wing electorate, in Europe at least. One suspects that unless some serious effort is made to rectify this situation in the near future, it may be too late. Britain's positive support for the American strike against selected Libyan targets in 1986 may not have been forthcoming had Britain been governed at the time by a Labor party.

NOTES

1. 28 August 1982. He was shot dead while waiting at a traffic light.

7

Targets and Techniques

Many potential terrorist targets are already classified as such by security and intelligence agencies. This, however, does not always ensure that such locations will be protected through adequate security precautions. Indeed, because of the very multiplicity of possible targets and the cost required to protect them (with police, military, or paramilitary forces), only a very few targets are beyond effective attack by even poorly equipped and ill-trained terrorists.

The possibility of protecting all possible targets pales further when one considers that terrorists often aim to seize or kill some specific individual, a symbolic representative of the enemy. Kidnapping poses more problems for the perpetrators than does assassination in the majority of situations, but the potential rewards are much higher, whether in terms of publicity, ransom payments, or political concessions. High-ranking government ministers, military personnel, and certain businessmen can be and are protected to varying degrees by their employers—usually the government or a larger corporation. However, the lower the status of the individual, the less protection is afforded. Thus a stage is reached where the safety of the individual rests only on his own awareness and ability and any general security measures that may be taken at airports, stores, and other public places. On the basic premise, then, that it is easier to kill a captain than a colonel, or an opposition member of parliament than the president or prime minister, the terrorist group will often choose such a middle-status individual rather than a more "logical" but better protected one.

In a modern society, needs and services are intricately interdependent. Take any one link out of this reciprocal network and the chain-reaction effects can be enormous. Because of this, the terrorist need not rely on force of arms alone to achieve his aims. Individuals sympathetic to a terrorist cause, but not themselves disposed toward actual violence, may volunteer or be recruited to disrupt and destabilize civil areas, while their paramilitary colleagues concentrate on violent destruction. In the course of this chapter, we will consider some of the areas in which the "white collar" terrorist may strike.

ACQUISITION OF DOCUMENTS

Military or other official personnel without politically significant rank or status may find themselves the target of terrorist attacks. These are often staged in an effort to secure usable intelligence or documentation. Most often such material will take the form of identity cards and/or pass or access codes. To this end, off-duty personnel in terrorist-active areas are sometimes lured into "ambush" scenarios. This is done typically by invitations to parties, sporting events, etc. In Northern Ireland, a popular IRA/INLA tactic has been to employ attractive female operatives, who arrange to be "picked up" by off-duty soldiers. At the end of an evening's drinking, for example, the soldiers are invited back to the supposed home of one of these young ladies "for coffee." At some point during the proceedings, the females make their excuses and leave the room. Their places are immediately taken by one or more armed terrorists who, having killed the soldiers, seize identity cards and (if applicable) other passes. Similar techniques have been employed in West Germany against NATO personnel.[1]

WATER AND FOOD SUPPLY

The potential for mass poisoning of a target populace seems high when one considers the design of most water-supply networks. Typically, we have a reservoir that fills naturally or is fed from remote sources, a system of pipes to carry the supply to purification plants and pump stations, and the distribution line from the plants and stations to the users. Such a system is difficult to protect at all times from all conceivable types of attack. The simple expedient of placing contaminants in the reservoir is a terrorist's obvious first choice. Most reservoirs are nothing more than large expanses of water, which often double as sailing and water-sport sites. Others may be underground, but are still accessible via air vents, inspection hatches, and pump room areas. Security, where it does exist at all at present, usually takes the form of periodic patrols that check locks on office and pump-room doors, etc. An individual, then, driving a truckload of highly toxic waste, stolen from a dump site elsewhere, could probably arrive, tip the material into the target reservoir, and drive away before anyone had a chance to stop him. At night, the incident might even pass completely unnoticed. Whether or not the waste were of sufficient concentration to cause serious harm would not matter as the publicity and fear once the incident were announced or discovered would cause enough damage. Terrorists could then play with public perception of the event. For example, they could issue a statement saying that, although the authorities denied any danger to users of the supply, there was indeed a high risk of cancer developing later. A variety of such ploys would be effective to instigate and amplify panic.

Threats to contaminate water supplies have been

made by radical groups and disturbed individuals from time to time. Nerve gas was to be the material used in one such threatened incident in New York in 1972.[2] Plutonium was threatened, again in New York, in 1985.[3] This latter attack was apparently actually carried out. Some press reports confirmed that plutonium had been found in a supply source, but that the quantities were so small as to be of no danger.

In point of fact, the quantity of material needed to contaminate a large reservoir beyond use is considerable. Millions of gallons of water are held in these systems and the dilutive effect is therefore tremendous. Also, the purification plant stands between reservoir and user (not that these plants can filter out all dangerous contaminants). However, the terrorist need only move up the supply chain a few steps and these problems are solved. One could contaminate a main branch pipe, for example, with much less toxic material. The number of victims would be smaller also, but only relatively. Even if the supply to a specific street or building were tampered with, an office complex perhaps, the numbers of people that could be killed or seriously harmed could run into the thousands. Simply walking into a building, locating one of the washrooms and attaching a self-sealing valve to a tap-supply pipe would suffice. Onto the valve, common since they are used for connecting washing machines, could be fitted a container of liquid contaminant, complete with syringe-type injector. The terrorist would need only minutes to perform the operation and would face hardly any risk of detection. Danger to the terrorist, if any, might stem from the manipulation of the contaminant.

The effect of such contamination would be far more dramatic than even a large conventional explosion. There would be large numbers of people dying or falling sick, and a subsequent search for the cause, including suspicion of water supplies, air-conditioning systems, and food sources. Widespread destruction and disruption could thus result through one simple terrorist act.

The contaminant employed in such attacks would probably be a biological agent, since these lend themselves well to liquid dissemination. There are other choices open to the terrorist, however: liquid chemical agents such as Tabun (GA), Soman (GD), or VX-type nerve agents. These could be used with only basic precautions to ensure the safety of the operative during the transport and injection stages. The range of biological agents suitable for dissemination through a water supply is large. If the intention were to disrupt rather than to kill, dysentery bacteria–noncontagious and rarely lethal–would be suitable. At the other end of the scale would be the extremely dangerous anthrax bacteria. There are some two thousand pathogenic bacteria, the effects of which range from sore throats and boils to agonizing death.[4]

The production of this type of microorganism is not difficult. For the most part, it requires only moisture, warmth, and simple food, such as sugar or broth. Furthermore, the bacteria can be stored in the liquid food material itself, where they will multiply rapidly. Chlorine in water supplies, however, offers protection against most bacterial agents (anthrax being a notable exception). Boiling also will kill many bacteria, although some are heat-resistant.[5]

Contamination of the food chain can also be achieved through the use of common bacteria. Here the most likely point of assault is a processing or packing plant. In such a plant, a huge volume of foodstuffs could be contaminated in a very short time, with relatively minor effort (perhaps including securing employment at the plant).

Even the threat of contamination, supported by a few well-placed samples on the shelves of large stores, can cause untold disruption. The Farley's baby food scare in England in December 1985 was caused by the illness of some infants whose last meals had included Farley products. It resulted in international media warnings being issued, the removal of literally millions of packages of Farley products from store shelves around the world, the closing down and examination of the manufacturing plant in England, and the screening of all employees for symptomless disease carriers. If such a campaign were conducted against a specific company over any length of time, it could actually cause the loss of so much public confidence that share values would plummet and the company could ultimately be destroyed. All this without the terrorists necessarily harming anyone.

For genuine contamination projects, a terrorist operative might well deliberately expose himself to contagious agents and secure employment within some food-producing establishment. He could move on before his illness or the effects of his actions became obvious.

CHEMICAL AND BIOLOGICAL TERRORISM

The relative ease with which chemical and biological agents can be transported and disseminated is well known. These factors, combined with the difficulties involved in detecting them and counteracting their effects, make them potentially more useful to the terrorist than a nuclear device. The spectrum of usable agents of this type is vast. It ranges from the type of nonlethal agents used in riot control—for example, dibenzoaxazepine (CR) or orthochloro-benzylidene-malononitrile (CS)—to deadly bacteria such as those causing anthrax, glanders, melioidosis and bubonic plague (pulmonary).

Chemical weapons are nonliving substances which kill, damage, or incapacitate. According to military authorities, agents that incapacitate are those that affect the mind, rendering the victim unable to concentrate or make decisions, or those that affect muscular coordination or motor activity. They do not normally cause death. Some of the more modern developments in this field have been agents that induce phobias or even "pleasant" effects comparable to those experienced by narcotic users.[6]

Biological agents are living microorganisms that cause disease in man, animals, and plants. An early example of biological warfare was the deliberate pollution by a retreating army of water sources with dead and rotting bodies. Many instances of this are recorded in military history. A current Soviet schoolbook explains a use of biological warfare by American soldiers to kill American Indians. The book tells us that the soldiers left blankets in which people had died of contagious diseases near reservations where they were sure to be found by the Indians.

Scientific developments have made it possible to manufacture biological agents under controlled conditions. Toxins should be mentioned here as they fall somewhere between chemical and biological categories. They are, in fact, extremely poisonous nonliving substances obtained from biological sources.[7] The poisons responsible for food poisoning are toxins, examples being: staphylococcal enteroozin, produced by the staphyloccus bacterium, and botulinum toxin, produced by clostridium botulinum. The latter toxin causes botulism. Even small doses of it produce symptoms within twelve to thirty-six hours and can prove fatal if left untreated, in which case there is a 70 percent mortality rate over a seven-day period.[8]

Both chemical and biological agents may be disseminated through the air. This is the method most likely to be selected by a terrorist group. An aerosol containing a contagious agent could be released at an airport with a view to spreading the disease internationally, or in a subway station in the hope of affecting a more localized target area. The term *localized* is used tentatively, of course, as the ultimate effects of such an attack could not be accurately predicted.

An indication of the initial coverage possible through airborne agents released in small quantities is provided by a test made in 1958 by the United States government. The contents of a single aerosol containing harmless bacteria released from a ship in San Francisco Bay was found spread to an area of some thirty square miles.[9] The abundance of air-conditioning equipment nowadays could also abet massive target penetration, and the cooling systems themselves used in many such networks are perfect breeding grounds for many biological agents. Indeed, natural outbreaks of Legionnaire's disease have been traced back to such installations.

Another alternative open to the terrorist is the contamination of telephone mouthpieces in public telephone booths. The warm, moist environment in and around the mouthpiece of a telephone in regular use is suitable for the growth and development of many bacteria. In spring 1985, a British survey of telephone booths in five major cities found four strains of communicable human disease and two types of fecal bacteria growing in the mouthpieces.[10]

It is interesting to note here that the terrorist can achieve a good deal without resorting to serious physical harm. As awareness grows among radical groups that *more* can be achieved by stopping just short of deadly action, a trend toward nonlethal terrorist techniques may develop. It is in this context that biological and chemical weapons could gain terrorist favor, especially because here a slight change in manufacturing process or decrease in dilution can once again turn the disruptive into the destructive. Medical agencies are not easily able to isolate the source of a disease. An outbreak of disease followed some time later by an announcement of responsibility by a terrorist group along with an ultimatum that if certain conditions are met, the outbreaks will stop, could easily bring about a more useful type of public reaction than a series of bomb attacks ever could.

A terrorist group might choose to restrict the agents used to those against which an immunity can be developed. In that way it could negate the risk to terrorist operatives themselves, ensuring their own immunity before commencing the actions. Even the use of such an agent could generate massive disruption. It would necessitate mass innoculation programs to prevent those not already infected from contracting the disease.

The chemical/biological option has obviously already been considered by terrorist groups on more than one occasion. In April 1975, fifty-three one-liter bottles of mustard gas were stolen from West German army bunkers, and the threat of an attack against Stuttgart and Bonn was made. At around the same time, some stolen nerve gas was recovered by Austrian police.[11] Articles in *SURVIVAL* magazine in 1976 mentioned reports of an Arab Pharmaceutical Congress offering support to the PLO in biological warfare training. In fact, as long ago as the nineteenth century, Irish terrorists considered using osmic gas against the houses of parliament. These and similar bizarre plans were never put into effect.[12] More recently, a British chemical company supplied Red China with four-hundred million dosage units of LSD (lysergic acid diethylamide 25). No official explanation has been given by the Chinese regarding what was done with the drug. The chances are that it is in storage somewhere. The amount of LSD involved here is truly massive, certainly enough to disable China's Soviet neighbors for more than ten hours. A couple of suitcases full of LSD, if added to the water supply, would be sufficient to incapacitate the entire United States for around eight hours (assuming everyone drank the water, of course). It is no secret that the U.S. government (via the CIA) and the Soviet government have undertaken serious research into the viability of employing LSD as a chemical warfare weapon. It is not beyond the realms of possibility, therefore, that the first we know of a Soviet offensive against the United States might be a sudden outbreak of smiling faces.

It is beyond the scope of this book to list all possible biological and chemical agents, their effects, and applicable countermeasures. Such information, however, is by no means useless. Any group opting to use such agents would, no doubt, first gain what it could through threats. It would probably issue pre-attack demands or warnings. Should this happen, the cost of protective equipment and suits would soar and their availability dwindle. The concerned reader, therefore, might wish to plan for such a contingency before the event.

STORES

Large stores are likely to remain popular terrorist targets for actual or bluff attacks, as the number of people affected in either case guarantees widespread fear and publicity. An attack may be made at any time of the year, but there are certain times that are more probable. These include holiday periods when the stores are more busy than usual. Christmas is a likely time for this very reason. Another factor makes Christmas "offensives" a popular terrorist tactic. Attacks at this time can have a strong dampening effect on the target community's spirits. Other likely times for attack are dates which coincide with some known terrorist anniversary, a day when there is a parade or other such event, or dates which coincide with or closely follow the announcement of some anti-terrorist or anti-"cause" measures by the target government. The risk of attack against some particular chain-store also increases if the chain owners' actions elsewhere could be construed as being supportive of some anti-terrorist cause. An American chain may operate in a foreign country in which there exists a strong anti-American "imperialism" movement, for example.

There is no practical way of preventing a determined terrorist attack against a large store without persuading shoppers to accept permanent war-like security screening at entrances and exits. After bomb attacks in England by the IRA in the 1970s, many stores employed "rent-a-guard" types to search shoppers as they entered the premises. While such techniques might deter the amateur bomber, they cannot be expected to defeat professional operatives. Professionals might well introduce explosive devices soldered into food cans or cast into blocks of cooking fat, neither of which can be searched properly without destroying it or rendering it useless; and both objects are obviously of a type that one could expect to find in the average shopping basket.

A more recent technique is to allow entering shoppers to bring parcels they have with them only as far as a "bagpark," built expressly for this purpose. This is a guarded area of the store away from the main shopping. The customer leaves the parcels and is issued a reclaim ticket. He or she is then allowed access to the store proper, carrying only empty store-provided carrier bags and certain (searched) personal articles.

The problem here is that the sheer volume of customers makes implementation of such techniques prohibitively expensive. If terrorist attacks increase, however, we may see enterprising individuals or groups establishing "terrorist-proof" shopping sites for up-market clientele prepared to pay higher prices for goods–or a membership fee–for the privilege of shopping in safety. (Entrepreneurs requiring further advice might care to contact the author!)

RESTAURANTS AND PAVEMENT CAFÉS

Pavement cafés, restaurants, food stands, and other such establishments are high-risk targets if located near government offices, foreign embassies, the headquarters of political groups, and so on. This is simply because of a belief on the part of the terrorists–valid or unfounded–that the staff from such places will frequent these establishments regularly. Consequently, lunch-times or after-work periods are to be considered the most dangerous for these kinds of places.

The attack itself might take the form of an exploding briefcase bomb left surreptitiously beneath a table or a burst of automatic-weapons fire from a passing vehicle. This latter technique is most applicable to out-of-doors establishments, of course. A bomb used in an outdoor location is likely to be a heavy nail or bolt device, calculated to generate large amounts of shrapnel in order to compensate for the dissipating effects of an explosion outside.

Conventional grenades are frequently used in such cases. The problem with this approach is that grenades can kill or injure anyone in the vicinity of the explosion. Thus they are not appropriate where the aim is to assassinate a specific individual. For the purposes of specific assault, other techniques are necessary. For example, there is the two-man assassination team, which enters the area and kills only the targeted person. In such instances, the target is not always known personally by the hit team. Hit team members will thus require a description or have to devise some other means of identification. Thus the targeted individual is often called by phone as he sits in the restaurant. When the target reacts to the telephone summons, the hit team moves in and kills him. This technique is often used by the IRA and ETA groups, but it frequently results in the death of innocents, as confusion over the names and/or description of the target is common. Individuals have also been killed in error because they responded to a "telephone for Mr. ———"announcement using only a last name. The trigger has been pulled, in other words, before the question "Is that *Alan* Smith?" can be asked. Thus an "Alan" has died in the place of a "Stephen" he never even knew existed.

Staff infiltration is also a possibility. The terrorist operative might secure employment at such a location with a view to overt assassination of a predetermined target when the opportunity presents itself; or with the intention of perpetrating a low-profile attack, such as one involving poison. In the latter case, responsibility for the murder may or may not be claimed, depending on the overall aims of the group. If the technique were to be used again, for example, the group might decline to announce its involvement for fear of stimulating additional security and screening measures.

CATERING SERVICES

An obvious move from the restaurant or food stand is catering companies. These may be infiltrated or even established with a view to general or specific assassination projects. The use of poisons in this context springs readily to mind. Civilian caterers are frequently employed by government departments or by government personnel on a personal basis for such occasions as weddings, birthdays, and so on. The dates of such events might be gleaned from establishment employees or the friends of friends invited to the event. In any case, the terrorist operative will have little difficulty in acquiring the information. Bulk caterers regularly employ short-term contract personnel for once-only functions. This provides for easy terrorist access.

BUSES AND BUS TERMINALS

"Highway robbery" operations, in which the bus is intercepted en route by armed terrorists and its passengers forced to hand over money, food, clothing, or other items of which the terrorists are in need, are not infrequent occurrences in underdeveloped, rural parts of the world. In such areas, the robbery aspect of the "attack" may also be supported by a propaganda dissemination exercise, the passengers being required to listen patiently to the terrorists' version of why they have chosen such a course of action, before being allowed to continue their journey.

Buses have also been hijacked in Northern Ireland by rioters–not all of whom have had any serious nationalist leanings–for use as barricades and vehicle bombs. During the Birmingham riots in England in 1986, buses were stoned and gas bombs thrown at them.

Buses and bus terminals which are known to be used regularly by military personnel fall into a special category. Quite often a private company will operate special buses at certain times of the month or the year to coincide with the leave arrangements of military bases. A security problem here is that unidentified baggage to be loaded on the bus is often left on the waiting-room floor or, more likely, outside at the pickup point. When the transport arrives, all luggage is loaded indiscriminately onto the bus. Very often, no check is made to determine to whom the luggage belongs. Consequently, a terrorist device hidden in an innocent-looking suitcase or military duffle bag will easily pass unnoticed. The drivers of such vehicles frequently take a hand in the loading themselves and will normally assume that an unattended item has been left by a passenger already on board. The device may be timed so as to explode during loading or after the journey has commenced.

ELECTRICITY

There are few things more disturbing than an unexpected interruption in the power supply. The psychological effect on a group of people suddenly finding themselves without light, heat, cooking facilities, radio and television broadcasts, and numerous other taken-for-granted aspects of an electricity-based society can be profound.

At home, fear and uncertainty regarding the cause and probable duration of the failure might be allayed for some time, especially if there is ready access to candles, batteries, and a gas stove. For passengers on an electric subway train or elevator, the effect will be more drastic. Panic would be likely in many situations. As an isolated incident or as part of some larger campaign, disruption of power service is likely to be high on the list of terrorist actions. It is, of course, a classic guerrilla tactic, used to harass or as a prelude to a more aggressive attack.

There are a variety of ways in which a terrorist group or lone operative might disable an electricity network.

All but the most primitive of supply systems include in their design a facility for rapid current diversion in the event of an overload or component failure. This may be fully automatic, manually switched, or a combination of both. The potential problem lies in the fact there are only a limited number of alternate paths by which the supply can be sent to a particular point. In remote areas, the destruction of a single cable may be enough to black out an entire town. In a major city, the effects would be more localized. Explosive charges placed at strategic points along the supply routes, while dramatic and effective, will be among the last techniques to be considered by the urban terrorist. Such actions are certain to provoke intense security-force reaction and result in more stringent preventive measures being introduced. Keeping the assaults low-key makes it difficult for the authorities to determine the cause of the failure and–in the absence of a statement–the motivation behind the attacks.

Having selected an isolated stretch of power line, the terrorist might shoot through it or short the circuit by firing lengths of wire across it and adjoining cables. The effect of this will be to force a shutdown of supply to that circuit from the main station or local substation. The area affected may or may not be resupplied almost immediately via a different circuit. In any event, the terrorists may now proceed to one or more of the transformers or other substations down-line from the break. These installations will, of course, now be without power. At these locations, few if any of which are protected by more than a simple fence, he can fire bolts or heavy rivets into the various components. There will be no immediate effect as the power is off, but when the broken cable is repaired and power to the circuit restored, the damaged, shorted transformers will create a series of new failures.

The time it would take to trace and repair or replace these units may be considerable. If, during the course of repairs, the same techniques were employed at different locations and the process repeated over an indefinite period, the strain placed on the power companies, local authorities, and police—who by this time would be under considerable pressure to stop the attacks—would be enormous. Local businessmen would be complaining about the loss of revenue, driving would become a nightmare because of outed traffic control systems, and the back-up battery systems in household and corporate burglar alarms would die because the main power was no longer charging them. Word would soon spread of this and looting could become rife. Police used to guarding the power network and searching for the perpetrators would be called back to control the escalating civil disturbances, leaving the terrorists room again to make more assaults, and so on.

It is certain that *Spetznatz* fifth columnists operating in the United States and Western Europe have identified weak points in national power supply systems and have contingency plans for destroying them prior to a Soviet-backed assault of a more serious nature.[13] The very nature of electricity supply networks makes them impossible to protect from attack in a practical manner. Redundancy, therefore, and emergency back-up systems are of some importance in negating the effects of any such attack.

SUBWAYS AND TRAINS

An attack on the electricity supply would also disrupt transportation systems such as trams and subway trains. The trams would stop, and people would complain and get off; but, assuming the level of traffic congestion generated by the stoppage was not too great, passengers could simply climb aboard buses. The reaction, then, would be annoyance rather than terror. For travelers on the subway, however, the situation would be much more serious. The potential consequences, as indicated by previous accidental power-supply interruptions, are terrible. Fear and panic resulting from the sudden entombment of thousands of people below ground would be bad enough; the hazards posed by opportunist criminals, however, make the scenario even more disturbing.

Most underground transit systems have some form of emergency lighting, but emergency back-up power is much more rare. Access to system-supply transformers is not difficult in most areas. Security measures—where they exist at all—generally are calculated to deter muggers and casual vandals rather than professional saboteurs.

ROADS AND STREETS

Streets are the arteries of any large city. Destroy, or even temporarily block, an important intersection, and a city can be brought to a standstill. Even on a good day in some big cities, with everything functioning as it should, it can take an hour to travel a matter of yards at rush-hour periods. (If ever there was a misnomer, it must be the term "rush hour.") The terrorist might attack traffic-control systems, lights, warning signals, or the street itself. In this latter case, the tried-and-tested method of abandoning one or more vehicles at some critical point shortly before a rush-hour period (and ensuring that they cannot easily be moved) would suffice.

Many major highways include sections which have other road systems or a rail bridge crossing above them. Such structures make it impossible for a helicopter to hover over the lower road and straight-lift away an obstructing vehicle. It is this type of location, therefore, where terrorists would place their obstacles. Similarly, much of a city's expressway network is raised, and only limited facilities exist for accessing certain parts of it with recovery and rescue vehicles. Police frequently have to enter the area on motorcycle and coordinate a mass reversing exercise. When traffic congestion causes delays of more than an hour (sometimes less), tempers, like engines, overheat; it is not unheard of for police to issue requests via the local radio stations to motorists in similar circumstances to remain calm. The problems caused by the deliberate abandonment of several vehicles, then, would be enormous.

To further delay restoration of traffic flow, the terrorist group might announce that the abandoned vehicles had been booby-trapped with explosives. This would immediately change the status of the whole affair and require painstaking and time-consuming effort on the part of reaction teams to confirm or refute the claim. Even a gag announcement would need to be taken seriously. The publicity, let alone the actual disruption, occasioned by such an event would be considerable–from the terrorist point of view, well worth the minimal effort involved.

An assault on the traffic-control systems requires only a modicum of ability and training on the part of the terrorist operative. Much of the electric cabling for highways runs alongside the road itself in conduits for ease of maintenance; but even where it is buried, it is seldom very deep. A simple incendiary device or a few blows with an insulated axe, and vast sections of traffic signals could be disabled. As any motorist will testify, the failure of even a single set of traffic lights can cause a dozen accidents in as many minutes. If the intersection affected is a particularly "fast" one, there may even be several deaths. Imagine the effect of a coordinated attack on the traffic-signal system encompassing several major intersections.

Contamination of the road surface is also a possibility. Substances damaging to rubber compounds are not difficult to find, and they may be spilled from the rear of a moving vehicle under cover of darkness. Even allowing for seepage and evaporation, sufficient amounts of material would remain on the road surface to be picked up by the tires of vehicles passing through the point some time later. Considering the number of vehicles that pass a given point on any major road, this simple act could literally affect thousands of vehicles before the contaminant could be reduced to safe levels.

RAILWAYS

Ticket-purchase areas and passenger waiting rooms, like their airport counterparts, are likely terrorist targets, simply because large numbers of people gather in them. Security at these locations is geared toward preventing ticket abuse, vandalism, or petty crime, rather than serious assaults by armed perpetrators. Unless a train is to cross international boundaries, there are no customs checks on passenger luggage. A terrorist team could enter any major rail terminal unchallenged, spray the assembled travelers with automatic-weapons fire, and stand a good chance of escaping unharmed. A bomb attack—with the device left in a luggage locker, perhaps—is always a possibility. The effort and planning needed to effect either kind of assault are minimal.

An attack against the railway-network or its signal-control system is another way to achieve massive disruption and/or inflict casualties on the target community. The technology involved in controlling today's high-speed trains is complex, and the slightest damage to any one of a hundred different component parts can shut down an entire network. The loosening of rail-mounting bolts, the severing of electric control cables, or the disabling of a railside signaling or switching unit are actions that could be accomplished by even a novice group. Elements of the Japanese Middle Core Faction in November 1985 staged a coordinated attack against the Tokyo rail system—one of the most advanced in the world. By cutting cables and burning electronic switching boxes, they succeeded in putting hundreds of miles of track out of use and halting the progress of some four-and-a-half million rush-hour travelers. These attacks—which included the firebombing of some stations—were carried out in support of railworkers seeking better employment conditions and benefits.[14]

Although massive damage can be caused by using simple techniques, it may not be long before the new technology employed in many rail systems comes under attack from sophisticated terrorist devices. Computer-controlled train-to-station signaling is becoming more widespread, and the techno-terrorist might easily construct a unit capable of interfering with such signals. Such a unit could be designed to give erroneous "all-clear" signals to a train driver or to indicate a train's position incorrectly on the electronic map in the control center. The more advanced the train and its control system, the more vulnerable it becomes to such attacks.

Train hijack is not unheard of, although it is the aircraft which generally finds itself the focus of such hijacking. Trains cannot readily be diverted to a point too far remote from the original destination, and there is an absolute limit to the distances which can be covered in them—the limit of available trackway. This, however, may cross international frontiers and the advantage of train hijack in the vicinity of such borders might, on occasion, outweigh the attendant disadvantages. Where the intention of the hijackers is to attract attention to a cause, the limitations will not be of great concern. A large number of people easily made captive and not easily rescued by security forces might be a sufficient magnet for the terrorist. Massive world attention was focused on a hijacked train in Holland in May 1977. The train was seized by seven South Moluccans as part of a campaign to secure greater independence from Holland for the South Moluccan islands. Fifty hostages were held on the train for several days. The Dutch government finally decided it had had enough and ordered a rescue attempt by marine commandos. Smashing their way into the rail car, the commandos screamed for the hostages to get on the floor and stay still as they sprayed machine-gun fire around them. Six Moluccans were killed, as were two hostages who had jumped to their feet in panic. The remaining hostages were rescued alive.[15]

COMMERCE

An attack on money supply may be considered by terrorist groups in the future. One of their initial objectives might not be to take away from the money supply, but rather to add to it by counterfeiting. Hitler considered such a technique on a grand scale and proposed flooding Britain with fake five-pound notes during World War II. The British at the same time planned to "bomb" German towns with counterfeit ration books. Neither project was ever successfully implemented.[16] The Croatian terror group Ustasha printed fake Yugoslavian 1000 Dinar notes; the LEHI–fighters for the freedom of Israel in Palestine–commissioned the forgery of government bonds.[17] Even the terrorists in India in the early part of this century tried to make counterfeit notes and coins. In the last case, however, the primary motive was to raise funds rather than to create chaos.[18]

The modern group inclined toward this course of action would face none of the problems a criminal counterfeiter would have in passing the money (which would probably be notes of large denomination). The intention being to disrupt rather than make a profit, the group might simply leave the notes in areas where finders could be relied upon not to announce their discovery to the authorities–poverty-stricken areas. There is no difficulty in making passable replicas of any currency, notes that might not stand up to close scrutiny by a bank official but that the average shopkeeper would take without hesitation. A well-funded group would be in a position to use manufacturing equipment very similar to that used at the mints and, although the type of paper used is said to be unavailable, after a note has been in use for some time the paper quality degrades rapidly anyhow. This effectively creates a wide range of paper grades.

Even producing poor-quality notes and distributing them widely—perhaps leaving bags of them in public places—would generate serious confusion, since hundreds of people might be caught trying to spend them. In the course of a single afternoon, a six-man team could easily "lose" hundreds of thousands of counterfeit dollars, the larger part of which would be kept and used by finders.

The counterfeiting of bearer bonds and other negotiable documents is another alternative. Commercial and savings banks, on being alerted that a percentage of their paper holdings might be counterfeit, would be unlikely to open up the vaults for independent verification. Much more probable is that they would simply dismiss the rumor as unfounded with the plan to recoup any losses via manipulative accounting. The motivation for them to do this is powerful, since even unsubstantiated rumors concerning the depreciation of a bank's assets is guaranteed to affect shareholder/customer confidence. In fact, banks often refuse to cooperate with investigative agencies on the trail of counterfeit documents for this very reason. A terrorist group employing such techniques would need to make a coordinated effort to place the false paper properly, but this would present little difficulty given the necessary financial backing.

A more rewarding technique than counterfeiting is that of "commercial colonization." In this approach, terrorist-backed teams either establish companies and develop them to maturity or buy in to existing companies. This will generate funds, of course, but its real purpose is to secure control over a large sector of a given economy. Although control of any large company is enough to give terrorists a foothold and negotiating platform, optimum choices would be companies employing large numbers of people and producing a product upon which the "enemy" society is dependent. If it is difficult to work in this way within the targeted country or area, the goal can still be achieved by securing control of companies in other areas that supply the targeted area. An ideal situation for the terrorists would be to control some really essential product, fuel-oil being, perhaps, the most critical.

Companies which support many hundreds of employees are in a powerful position to influence local government. A terrorist-controlled company or group of companies would have little difficulty in applying pressure on officials to help achieve certain aims. These need not be particularly drastic. They could conceivably include special status for an ethnic minority group—preferential housing schemes, special health-care arrangements, etc.; or even the imposition of sanctions on an "enemy" regime, such as the banning of goods made in a particular country, extra duties on goods imported from it, and so on. A terrorist group might even achieve aims of this type simply by infiltrating shipyard areas and inciting other workers to refuse goods from certain areas.

If control of large international companies were achieved, a failure on the part of government to concede to certain "requests" could result in the terrorist-controlled directors deliberately ruining the company and its interests. It may even be the case that the company has been dealing almost exclusively with terrorist-allied businesses or the backing regime itself, as part of the operation, rather than through necessity. In this instance the withdrawal and relocation of trade arrangements could seriously damage a target country's economy. The mere threat of this, of course, and politicians' fear of being blamed for loss of jobs and revenue would be sufficient motivation for them to work extremely hard at accommodating the requests. Employees of such companies, also, for fear of losing their jobs, would be loathe to express strong opinions contrary to those of their employers. Even if they do not agree with the "new" political aims of the company, in the vast majority of cases, they would put the well-being of themselves and their families first. It may be, of course, that the ultimate aims of the infiltrators and their backers are not extreme at all. In this case, they might find in the company employees a further source of active personnel.

The PLO, under the direction of Yasser Arafat, has secured control of countless commercial and industrial interests in the Middle East and the United States. PLO-backed companies also own an airline and a hotel in the Maldive Islands and many farms and manufacturing businesses in Africa. Up until 1982, the PLO dominated Lebanon economically, and an estimated 10,000 people worked for companies owned by the group. The same commercial techniques have been applied in Jordan where the Palestinian group operates fruit plantations, transport companies, and textile mills. Close liaison and cooperation with the PLO is maintained by the companies–when a bank in Amman announced recently its intention to construct a new building, the PLO insisted that Palestinian companies get the contract. Or else, warned the PLO, its substantial deposits would be withdrawn from the bank.[19]

While this type of campaign seems possible only for state-sponsored groups, one should remember that several well known "free-lance" terrorists have had legitimate access to vast sums of money. Feltrinelli, millionaire publisher; "Carlos," son of a millionaire lawyer; and Patricia Hearst, the kidnapped heiress-granddaughter of millionaire William Randolph Hearst, who "turned" and joined her captors to become the guerrilla "Tania."[20]

INDUSTRY

We saw in our discussion of training that many extremist political groups, especially those in Europe, instruct selected cadres in the skills of strike provocation and industrial disruption. It is by using the time-tested methods referred to in that discussion that future activists may seek to undermine the industrial strength of a nation. Of course, to some extent these techniques are constantly in use. The miners strike of 1985 in England is a good example of how a hard core of militants can influence the opinions and actions of the majority. In addition to the damage caused to the industry, many people were seriously injured during this dispute in clashes between striking miners and police. Miners who refused to strike were assaulted or had their homes burnt to the ground, their families were threatened with death, and one man was killed when a concrete block was dropped from a bridge onto the windshield of a taxi in which he was traveling. Imagining that such incidents do not have terrorist causes would be a mistake.

Many steps have already been taken to limit the incidence of total strikes in industry: no-strike agreements made before a labor force is contracted, profit-sharing schemes and bonus payments for uninterrupted work periods, and others. These measures have all served to tighten the relationship between worker and employer. The individual whose monthly paycheck is determined by his own efforts and those of his colleagues is unlikely voluntarily to sacrifice it in the hope of making some political point. Agitators and extremists who are not already established will find it more difficult in the future to secure support in "bringing down the management." As links between management and labor draw tighter, doing so will bring down the workers as well. Not all companies take such measures, however. In companies where a strong militant group exists, it may still simply use the democratic process against moderate members of a negotiating committee to take control. It may then throw any prior agreements to the wind.

It is well known that certain extremist groups maintain a paid body of agitators, whose task is simply to secure employment in selected areas of industry and cause as much chaos as possible. Many of these operatives hold degrees in political science, psychology, or other disciplines, yet obtain unskilled jobs as fitters and assemblers. From this position, they disseminate anti-management propaganda. Most of these activists remain only long enough to generate disruption and discontent and then move on to another plant or factory. Some, however, will be long-term employees, whose task will be low-profile sabotage actions. These individuals often spend some considerable time establishing their credentials as loyal and trusted employees. They are, therefore, far more dangerous than their short-term, loud-mouthed counterparts. Promotion schemes may lead this type of activist into supervisory or even management positions. Here, perhaps in the capacity of a quality-control supervisor, for example, the operative could deliberately pass substandard products (perhaps made by colleagues on the shop floor). In an auto plant, these might be brake parts which would fail after a short in-service period. This would necessitate expensive recalls and repairs and undermine customer confidence.

Infiltrators of the high-tech industry could cause untold damage and generate huge security problems simply by seeing that every batch of equipment destined for a defense-related user contained a higher than normal percentage of faulty components. Service companies providing support for computer users continue to grow steadily in number and this may prove another avenue of access for the terrorist operative. Many primary users are blissfully ignorant of precisely how their systems operate, and this fact can be exploited by the knowledgeable infiltrator employed as a service/repair man. Information might be extracted from computer systems under cover of repair or the systems might be sabotaged. Simple knowledge of details of a system's operating procedures would prove valuable to any terrorist group. The Royal Ulster Constabulary computer in Northern Ireland, which holds information pertaining to thousands of known and suspected terrorists and undercover operatives, was installed for security reasons by experts from Vancouver, Canada.[21]

We saw in considering the funding of terrorist groups that many such groups establish legitimate businesses as a cover for their operations and as a means of generating and laundering funds. With this in mind, it becomes apparent that the dangers posed to clients of those companies is great. Terrorist-backed construction companies—a common cover—may find themselves in a position to sabotage some structure which they have been contracted to build or repair. Deliberately building in flaws is one possibility, delayed structural time bombs which, when discovered at some later date, necessitate expensive and disruptive repair efforts. Intimate knowledge of a building, gained in building it, may also prove useful to the group in future operations. An extreme but workable possibility would be the building in of surveillance or explosive devices that could be operated remotely after a suitable settling-down period had elapsed. Modern electronics make it possible to construct a radio-controlled device which could be hidden in a wall and triggered at any time up to five years later. A readily available book details how to cast incendiary material in brick form.* This would be ideally suited for the terrorist builder. It is conceivable that an entire wall could be peppered with such castings which burn at temperatures high enough to defeat metal targets. Even the claim by a terrorist group that it had done such a thing, once a link between the group and the construction company had been established, could lead to expensive, disruptive, and demoralizing searches. An explosive version of the incendiary brick—replete with cast-in radio-controlled detonator and battery power source—is a possible variant.

On a very basic level, the terrorist group may simply threaten existing areas of industry in the manner dem-

---

**Improvised Munitions Black Book Volume 3* (Cornville, Arizona: Desert Publications, 1982; also available from Paladin Press). The material in the cited publication was originally developed for the U.S. Special Forces by The Frankford Arsenal in 1963.

onstrated by the IRA in 1985, when they succeeded in halting construction of police and military establishments by threatening to kill employees if they continued to work on the sites. So effective did this technique prove that the authorities were forced to consider bringing in workers from the mainland and giving them constant military protection.[22]

The brick-casting technique is becoming quite popular among certain terrorist groups. Pentrite is, by all accounts, the most suitable type of explosive for this particular application. Impossible to detect by conventional X-ray methods, any innocent-looking object may be cast from a mixture of pentrite and some other materials to produce a deadly, yet inconspicuous, piece of ordnance. A plate, for example, or a ceramic wall decoration—of a type which anyone might bring back from a trip abroad—could be cast in such a manner so that the detonator mounting sockets looked like screw fixing points. Such items could easily be transported through border checkpoints and onto aircraft without arousing suspicion. In the latter case, a second party would carry the detonator(s) disguised as some other innocent item (a pen or lipstick, for example) on-board an aircraft. The two component parts could then be assembled on-board and an attack initiated.

Cold-cure resin mixes are another method by which the terrorist can hide an explosive device. These mixes are used in the making of chess sets and the like. With the addition of readily available metal powder, the normally clear resin can be made to look and feel like solid metal. A thorough physical examination of an object made from this material is impossible without actually breaking the item apart. X-ray devices could be defeated by virtue of the fact that the item would appear to be solid metal if properly constructed, and explosive sniffing units would be defeated since the explosive material itself would be hermetically sealed inside the object.

The temperatures reached by this resin material as it sets are not sufficient to set off modern, plastic-type explosives. Nor is it sufficient to cause a modern electric detonator to explode. A complete package, then, of explosive and radio-controlled detonator could be sealed into some innocent-looking object and carried with minimal risk of detection to its target. The radio signal which would trigger the detonator would pass through the resin mix only if the metal content were not too great. A way around this potential screening problem, however, would be for the terrorist to extend the "antenna" of the detonator so that it contacted the surrounding metal "shell" of the object. The whole thing would then act as an antenna.

SHIPS

As the seizure of the Italian cruise ship *Achille Lauro* off the Egyptian coast in 1985 confirmed, seagoing vessels are as vulnerable to terrorist aggression as are airplanes. Indeed, as air security continues to improve, the risks to shipping become greater. The planning and effort required to seize even the largest of passenger vessels is far less than that needed to successfully hijack an aircraft. Not the least significant reason for this is that an airplane may be accessed only at its points of departure and arrival, while a ship may be intercepted and boarded at any point en route. Weight and size restrictions applicable to aircraft baggage—let alone any effective security measures—preclude the introduction onto an airliner of any but the most portable and concealable of weapons. The type of luggage taken by passengers on lengthy sea voyages is subject to far fewer limitations. For no apparent reason other than tradition, the security applied to cruise passengers in the vast majority of situations is poor, to say the least. Nonpassengers are regularly allowed on board by many companies. Although they are requested to leave shortly before departure, few will deny that this visiting privilege is often abused. Any subsequent manifest checks are easily avoided simply by staying out of the way. It is a known fact that on the larger vessels, friends of crew and passengers regularly travel free simply by keeping a low profile. The sheer numbers of new faces on-board a vessel at any given time reduce the risk of detection to almost zero. The more numerous the ports of call and the more frequent the change of passengers, the greater the chances of unauthorized persons getting and remaining aboard.

There is no real need, of course, for the terrorist to employ such means. Unless he is a known and wanted criminal unable to secure false travel documents, he can easily purchase a ticket in the normal fashion. Weaponry can be taken on-board hidden in luggage or, if crew-infiltration techniques have been employed, under cover of linen and food supplies.

Another possibility is that the terrorist group divides into two teams. One team joins the voyage from its onset and immediately sets about pinpointing strategic areas (bridge access routes, radio rooms, etc.) in readiness for the arrival of the second team, which intercepts the vessel en route, bringing along the required weaponry.

The *Achille Lauro* was not the first vessel to be hijacked by terrorists. On February 11, 1963, FALN operatives seized the cargo ship *Anzoategue* and radioed propaganda messages back to an amazed Venezuelan audience. In this case, the operatives had stowed away and no one was injured.[23]

Oil or LPG (liquid propane gas or liquid petroleum gas*) tankers might also be targeted in a terrorist operation–an RPG (rocket-propelled grenade) attack or assault with an explosive-packed "boat bomb" are two real possibilities. Such an attack would likely occur as the vessel was unloading cargo in order that massive publicity could be guaranteed. The storage-terminal complex itself might consequently also be destroyed

---

*In the United States, more commonly termed LNG, or liquified natural gas.

as fires spread. The final result–in terms of physical damage and revenue loss–would be enormous. The boat-bomb technique might involve a suicide "pilot," who would navigate the floating weapon to its target and detonate it manually; or it might be rigged to explode on impact. An alternative is the use of radio-controlled vessels. The technology involved in attaching a radio-remote system to a small motorboat, for example, is not overly complex. Left- and right steering and power increase and decrease are all that is required. The use of model boats is a technique not to be overlooked either. A large model could easily be adapted to contain enough explosive to seriously damage a full-size vessel. If the target vessel were unloading petroleum products at the time of the attack, an incendiary or explosive device could be used to trigger a chain reaction. The fumes present during loading and unloading of vessels carrying gasoline are great. This fact, plus the simultaneous presence of inflammable liquids atop the water surface surrounding the vessel, would almost guarantee the desired result.

NUCLEAR TERRORISM

The possibility that terrorists may one day construct a nuclear device has long been the concern of many. In theory at least, the task is not a difficult one given elementary knowledge of the field, suitable manufacturing facilities, and, of course, sufficient fissionable material. It is securing enough fissionable material to sustain a chain reaction–the critical mass–that presents the techno-terrorist with his greatest difficulty. If too small a quantity is used, more neutrons escape from the surface of the reaction area than are being created at its center, and the chain reaction stops. It is the massive energy release caused by such a chain reaction that gives the nuclear device its devastating power. It begins when one atom of uranium 235 (U-235) or plutonium splits under the impact of a neutron. The atom splits into two fragments and releases more neutrons, which in turn split more atoms, and so on. Each stage of this reaction takes only a millionth of a second to occur.

If the required amount of Uranium 235 is obtained, incorporating it into a bomb is not at all difficult to do. Let us assume that the minimum critical mass is about eleven kilograms. That amount of the material not only need not–but *must* not–be present until detonation is required. If it *were,* than an unwanted spontaneous chain reaction would start. With this in mind, the material would be fashioned into the bomb in two parts. Each of these parts in isolation would be "subcritical." The next design consideration is how these two subcritical parts can be brought together in an instant. There are a couple of ways this can be achieved by employing conventional weaponry in an unconventional way, but rather than give specific details–which are available in more specialized works anyway–we will generalize. In the original Hiroshima bomb, a "wedge" of U-235 was fired by an explosive charge down a large gun-barrel-type assembly inside the bomb casing into a "ball" of U-235. In the Nagasaki bomb, a sphere of plutonium was packed around a central core of beryllium (which emits neutrons). The size of the sphere was such that enough neutrons escaped from its surface to stop the plutonium and the beryllium from going critical. Upon detonation, a conventional explosive smashed the sphere of uranium onto the beryllium. This latter design is still the basis of most nuclear and thermonuclear weapons and is likely to be the design chosen by terrorists should they ever develop such a capability.

The uniform detonation of the conventional explosive surrounding the fissionable material is the most technically demanding aspect of the system, but a simple computer program–well within the scope of any home micro–will provide the required detonator spacing details based on amount of material, etc. The terrorist group working without the support of a wealthy agency or state is unlikely to be able to replicate the finer points of a mass-produced weapon; but it is foolish to pretend that construction of a nuclear device is for some reason prohibitively complex for anyone but official agencies. The problem of securing the fissionable material is the only one that cannot be readily overcome. Some estimates conclude that there is a 50-percent risk of death in stealing such material and a 30-percent risk of death to those manufacturing weapons with it. Whether or not such risks would be of concern to a fanatical group is unknown. Conceivably, those inclinded to build such a weapon might simply look on the death of team members as a necessary evil.

The risk of some unstable regime acquiring a nuclear capability and either offering it for terrorist use overtly or, as is more likely, pretending that fissionable material had been stolen when in reality it had been handed over freely, is real. Khadafi has been trying for some time to buy a nuclear capability; but so far even his allies in a position to oblige have declined to make it available to him, primarily because of United States pressure. If a point were reached, however, where a potential supplier concludes he has more to gain than lose from ignoring United States and other Western governmental pressure, the shape of international politics could change enormously. While Middle Eastern states will continue to attract interest and suspicion from concerned quarters, other countries capable of producing—and therefore supplying—nuclear material and weapons grow steadily in number. In November 1985, Indian Foreign Minister Bali Ram Bhagat stated that his country's arch rival, Pakistan, had produced enough weapons-grade nuclear material to make three to five bombs.[24]

Weapons-grade material is the operative phase in the context of nuclear weapons. While the fear that a terrorist group might steal uranium from a nuclear power plant is well founded, complex centrifuge equipment would still be required to enrich such material and make it suitable for weapons manufacture. Natural uranium (unenriched), as supplied to many nuclear facilities, contains only around 0.7 percent of the fissile U-235. The rest is non-fissile U-238, an isotope. An isotope is simply a variety of the element identical in every way except for the mass of its atom. U-238 does not split easily, and, regardless of how much of it is present in one lump, natural uranium cannot sustain a fission reaction.

In a nuclear power plant, the natural uranium is enriched, probably using gas-centrifuge techniques in which uranium hexafluoride is subjected to high-speed rotation, resulting ultimately in the separation of U-235 and U-238. The U-235 will then be turned into usable fuel by converting it into uranium oxide. In the traditional system, this powdered uranium oxide is next compressed into small pellets which are loaded into hollow rods, ready for inserting into the reactor. All reactors, during the course of their operation, create the fissile isotope plutonium 239, and it is this material which is of interest to the terrorist. "Spent" fuel rods are removed from reactors and subjected to reprocessing in which the fuel is separated into three main streams—unburned U-235, plutonium 239, and waste products. The uranium and plutonium may be recycled for use in new fuel rods, and the waste must be stored until its lethality declines to "safe" levels. To reach such a level can actually take seven hundred years or more.

An extreme but possible variation on the traditional steal-material-and-make-a-bomb scenario is that the terrorist group constructs its own crude "reactor" with a view to causing a deliberate meltdown. We have seen that natural uranium contains only a small percentage of fissionable material and that in the normal course of events the proportion of its fissile isotope is increased using gas-centrifuge enrichment methods. Another way of achieving this increase in the fissile isotope, however, is known as moderation. This is worth consideration here if only because in a crude form the technique is frighteningly simple.

Neutrons produced by fission travel extremely fast and therefore tend to escape before they can cause further fission (the chain reaction). A fast neutron can be slowed down by forcing it to bounce repeatedly off some lighter element known as a moderator. By slowing the neutrons, the chances of them hitting other uranium nuclei and causing *them* to split are increased. One such moderator is graphite. It is the moderation principle using graphite which the techno-terrorist could employ. An assembly comprising graphite blocks drilled to take small containers of stolen uranium and cadmium control rods is essentially all that would be required. (There is no difficulty in obtaining graphite or cadmium.) The graphite "reflects" (moderates) the neutrons spontaneously produced by the small amount of U-235 present in the uranium material, and the cadmium rods absorb them. If the cadmium rods are withdrawn, the number of neutrons available to cause fission increases tremendously, and eventually a point will be reached where the reaction becomes self-sustaining. If this escalating release of energy is not stopped it will run out of control and cause a "meltdown." In a nuclear reactor, this controlled generation of fission is used to produce heat that, via a heat-exchange system of gas or water, makes steam, which is used to generate electricity.

An interesting change occurs within the pile, however, in the hitherto non-fissile U-238. Bombarded by neutrons from the U-235 it becomes a new and infinitely more dangerous material–Pu-239, the plutonium isotope. Were the terrorist group to embark on such a project, it would not need to be concerned with the technical difficulties of chemically extracting the plutonium, but could simply leave the pile to melt down, releasing large quantities of deadly radiation. Alternatively, if the process were stopped before meltdown, the highly enriched material could be distributed via conventional explosions or even manually. The contamination potential of even minute amounts of plutonium is considerable and the group in possession of such material would undoubtedly find itself in a powerful bargaining position indeed. A terrorist group seeking to "prove" its nuclear capability but not desiring to take too many of the attendant risks might simply irradiate an object or area and notify the media. When subsequent tests showed that the radiation present was indeed that associated with weapons-grade material, it would be difficult in the extreme for any authority not to take threats and demands issued by the group seriously.

Emergency-reaction teams exist in most Western countries, their tasks being to trace radiation sources in the event of a nuclear threat by terrorists. Aircraft and sophisticated detection equipment are available to the United States Nuclear Emergency Search Team, as, probably, are rats, for these are the only animals that can smell radiation. If a device were found as the result of a search—which, given that such a device would be extremely well shielded to defeat such efforts, is unlikely—the ensuing action would have to be very carefully considered. Political "face" and long-term consequences would take priority over concern for potential loss of life. If an effective terrorist nuclear capability did emerge, it could easily mean an end to conventional governmental control of world affairs as we know it. Nations would be obliged to bargain on equal terms with relatively small groups of extremists or engage in open hostilities. At the very least, a private-sector nuclear capability would enable groups intent on expansion to seize small countries with far less vulnerability to existing "superpowers" than at present.

The fear of nuclear terrorism has provoked many stringent control measures in relation to material supply, processing, and disposal. The French announced in 1977 that they had developed a safe way of making nuclear-reactor fuel that could not be used to make explosives. A technique used in the 1960s kept the material in a nuclear fuel recycling plant so radioactive that it could not be stolen. Armed personnel—military and/or civilian—are present at all establishments that are considered high-risk targets, and rapid-reaction teams exist that would successfully defeat any terrorist attempt at penetration and theft.[25] Whether or not aggressive actions could be defeated without serious loss of life and contamination of a wide area is open to debate. Even a rocket attack against a convoy of military weapons is possible. Although such weapons are never in a ready-to-fire state when being transported from point A to point B, and, therefore, the risk of a nuclear *explosion* resulting from such an attack is minimal, damage to warheads would certainly cause the release of radioactive contaminants.

As an aside, if a nuclear capability were developed by some terrorist group, the step from nuclear fission to fusion weaponry would not be particularly large. All the research and development would have been already completed!

We might consider briefly the technology of the H-bomb. In essence, the power of the H-bomb is obtained not from the splitting, or fission of the atom, but rather from the fusion or combination of two hydrogen isotopes—deuterium and tritium. An idea of the technology involved in such weapons can be gained by considering the operation of a typical air-drop bomb, the WE 177, which is currently used by the RAF (British Royal Air Force). In this system, a hollow sphere of conventional explosive surrounds a shell of beryllium and uranium in the center of which is a ball of solid plutonium. The plutonium is plated with twenty-four karat gold to prevent oxidization. Upon detonation, the explosive crushes the beryllium-uranium shell down onto the plutonium and the weapon goes critical. The heat and radiation are focused onto a large, wedge-shaped cylinder of hydrogen-rich lithium. In the milliseconds before the bomb is destroyed, the temperatures within it reach those found on the sun, around one hundred million degrees centigrade. Then fusion begins.

This weapon, in common with similar types, has a mechanism for adjusting the size of the explosion that externally resembles the temperature control found on domestic stoves. This is the so-called "dial-a-yield." On setting "1," small, localized targets may be destroyed—bridges, for example. On setting "4," the yield will flatten entire cities. The H-bomb, then, is really a bomb within a bomb, and a less-sophisticated design might consist of an atom bomb within a uranium case that is itself contained within a normal bomb casing. The fusion not only creates a huge explosion, but also releases enormous amounts of radioactive-fission products. These can create dangers of contamination for years, literally, as some elements—strontium 90, for example—can be taken up by the food chain and cause cancer in humans.

An alternative which might be considered by terrorist groups is the securing of quantities of low-level/medium-level radioactive material for use in blackmail or contamination projects. A potential source of such material is the liquid-waste discharge systems which are often to be found leading from nuclear plants into rivers or—if the level of contamination is slightly higher—the sea. The radiation levels in such discharge systems are constantly monitored and consequently rarely ever exceed officially safe limits. However, these "safe" levels are frequently greater than normal background radiation by up to two hundred times and will, therefore, register strongly on radiation-detection equipment. Similarly, areas of soil or sand near to discharge points will contain even significantly higher levels of radioactivity due to cumulative effects.

Employing this knowledge, a terrorist group could construct a "nuclear device" containing only irradiated soil and inform the media of its demands. To "prove" that its threat to detonate a nuclear device is real, the group might invite media representatives to examine electronically the "weapon" with radiation detection meters. The material present would certainly indicate radioactivity and, armed with this "evidence," media representatives would no doubt give massive publicity to the situation. Using such material to irradiate a rented office or apartment and then claiming that a weapon had been constructed might also generate serious concern from the authorities, who would have to work very hard indeed to satisfy a worried public that this could not possibly have happened.

NOTES

1. Various sources, including conversations with British military personnel.
2. *New York Daily News,* 14 February 1977.
3. Various newspaper reports and magazine articles.
4. From training notes in author's possession.
5. Ibid.
6. Ibid.
7. Ibid.
8. From military biological and chemical warfare training notes in author's possession.
9. Duncan Long, *Chemical/Biological Warfare Survival* (Wamego, Kansas: Long Survival Pubs., 1980), p. 2.
10. Tests conducted at the Queen Mother Hospital, Glasgow, and revealed on British national television in 1985.
11. Walter Laqueur, *Terrorism* (Weidenfield and Nicolson, 1977), p. 231.
12. Ibid., p. 228.
13. *Spetznatz,* or *spetsnaz,* is an abbreviation for the Russian term *spetsaznacheniya,* "special designation." Spetznatz teams can be considered the equivalent of Western special forces units. Spetznatz operations pre-

ceded the Soviet invasions of Hungary, Czechoslovakia, and Afghanistan. Indigenous fifth-columnists have access to radio equipment facilitating communication with Moscow. They are allocated specific targets and strike in support of regular forces. Spetznatz units regularly stage practice assaults on mock-ups of foreign targets, for example, 10 Downing Street (official residence of the British Prime Minister), government offices in Whitehall, radar stations, nuclear establishments, etc. They are also known to have mock-ups of cruise missiles, which they practice disabling with plastic explosive charges especially designed not to cause a nuclear explosion.

Several of the diplomats expelled from Britain in the autumn of 1985 are known to have been Spetznatz recruiters. Despite the sneers of many pro-Soviet politicians, the threat is real enough in the minds of the British government to have warranted the largest military exercise ever to be staged in Britain. The exercise, Brave Defender, begun in September 1985, was the largest mobilization of military personnel to be seen in the country since World War II. Its purpose was specifically to test the home defenses against assault by Spetznatz regulars in combination with indigenous sympathizers.

14. Various radio and newspaper reports throughout November 1985.

15. J. Bowyer Bell, *A Time of Terror* (New York: Basic Books, 1978), pp. 175–78, 273.

16. David Kahn, *Hitler's Spies* (New York: Macmillan, 1978), p. 341.

17. Walter Laqueur, p. 87.

18. Ibid., p. 87.

19. *London Times,* 9 December 1985.

20. J. Bowyer Bell, pp. 46–47, 111.

21. For a long while the RUC used the army computer at Thiepval Barracks, Lisburn. Their new computer is at the Knock Road headquarters, Belfast. The computer files contain not only details on individuals, but

also information concerning the color of living room furniture, make of television, type of car driven, and so on. The collection of such details may seem a futile exercise, but it can often speed the identification of an individual in a search-and-question situation. One also suspects that operators feel loath to see computer memory space unused. For obvious reasons, the RUC will not confirm the computer installation details.

22. At the time of writing this situation is still going on. Several of the large British contractors subsequently approached have declined to assist, as they have already received IRA death threats. Even with an offer of extra "danger money" and a guarantee of military protection, the British government is finding it had to resolve the problem. It may transpire that more troops will be deployed in the province to try to stabilize the situation. This would run contrary to current policy, as the British are trying hard to "Ulsterize" the whole Irish affair.

23. J. Bowyer Bell, pp. 65–66, 131.

24. Various newspaper reports in England during November 1985.

25. The activities of the "peace protesters," especially in Europe, near and occasionally *in* nuclear facilities, give cause for concern. However, the ability of the protesters to get into certain facilities should not be taken as an indication that security is nonexistent. Overreaction on the part of the police or military is precisely what these activists hope to encourage; consequently, the facility personnel are instructed to keep a very low profile. The "peace camps" near United States nuclear-missile bases in England and elsewhere are obvious choices for terrorist infiltration and are therefore bound to be similarly infiltrated by intelligence-agency personnel.

A percentage of the individuals encamped at such places are obviously there with the sole intention of collating useful intelligence on the target facility for possible subsequent use by an enemy regime or indigenous activist group. While many of the assaults currently undertaken by such people are little more than fence-cutting exercises, one wonders how many would be prepared to seize an opportunity for serious sabotage, of weapons systems, for example, should the opportunity to do so present itself.

It is no secret that many of the "peace groups" issue printed information explaining how cruise-missile carriers can be prevented from deploying. In parts of England where the missiles are stored, it is possible to watch the activist supporters of such groups holding their own exercises along with those of the military. While the military personnel practice deploying to launch sights quickly and efficiently, the "peace people" simultaneously practice intercepting them and disrupting their convoys.

The protesters employ radio communication to pass on details of the convoy's movements to protest groups in other parts of the area in order that a "reception committee" might be ready for them. CND (Campaign for Nuclear Disarmament) elements operating under the banner *Cruisewatch* have also issued telephone numbers of key defense establishments and, indeed, those of the Defense Ministry itself. In a military emergency, the activists intend to tie up these lines with calls, thus further disrupting the British capability to react to a given situation quickly and without confusion.

In an effort to avoid the attentions of this and similar activist groups, and as part of conventional security measures, the sites of many important nuclear facilities are omitted from national maps of England. An example of such an establishment is the Royal Ordnance Factory at Burghfield, near Reading, England. This factory builds and maintains nuclear weapons. It is the site at which two Hungarian intelligence officers were arrested for taking photographs in April 1976. (The location of this establishment is already widely known, due to television and newspaper reports.)

8

Aircraft and Air Terminals

Aircraft and air terminals have become the traditional targets of the modern-day terrorist. Since this area is of such great importance in any consideration of terrorism, it is worth its own chapter.

The first recorded incident of a commercial-aircraft hijacking occurred in 1932 in Peru when an F7 was seized by rebel soldiers during a military coup. The aircraft, flown by an American, Byron D. Richards, was used to drop pamphlets.[1] It was to be some time, however, before the publicity-attracting potential of "skyjacking" was fully realized and exploited. In the interim period, violence and loss of life were the exception rather than the rule.

An average of five aircraft a year were hijacked between 1945 and 1950, predominantly by individuals seeking to escape to the West from Iron Curtain areas. In August 1966, an interesting incident occurred. In that month, an Argentinian Airlines flight to Rio Gallegos was seized and diverted to a little-known island group in the South Atlantic—the Falklands. After a somewhat precarious landing on a local racetrack, the hijackers, a group of Argentine nationalists led by Maria Christina Varrier, planted Argentine flags, announced their claim to the islands, and then waited with the rest of the passengers and crew until the monthly mail boat arrived to take them home again.[2]

Throughout the 1960s, the instances of aircraft hijacking grew steadily and peaked in 1969 with 91 such incidents.[3] A large number of these hijackings centered on Cuba, which was continuing to attract post-revolution revolutionaries, lunatics, and criminals alike. The Cuba connection was effectively shut down in 1969 with the introduction of the United States–Cuba antihijacking accord.[4] Media coverage of the numerous incidents had, however, ensured that the Cuban connection would remain synonymous with hijacking for many years to come.

A more ominous incident occurred in July 1968 in a very different part of the world, when a three-man team from the PFLP (Popular Front for the Liberation of Palestine) seized an El Al flight and diverted it to Algiers. Most of the passengers and crew were held until the Israeli government agreed to release imprisoned Arab terrorists. Immediate additional security measures were initiated by the Israelis to prevent the occurrence of similar incidents. These measures were to herald the arrival of the now legendary El Al antiterrorist precautions. It has been the Middle Eastern groups who have remained at the forefront of aircraft-related terror since that time, as a partial catalogue of incidents from that quarter to date illustrates:[5]

1. July 22, 1968. An El Al flight out of Rome is hijacked by PFLP and diverted to Algiers.
2. December 26, 1968. The PFLP attacks an El Al aircraft on the ground at Athens.
3. February 18, 1969. A PFLP commando team attacks an El Al aircraft during takeoff from Zurich.
4. August 29, 1969. A TWA flight out of Rome is seized by the PFLP and diverted to Damascus.
5. February 21, 1970. A PFLP bomb explodes onboard SwissAir flight bound for Israel. Forty-seven passengers killed.
6. September 6, 1970. The PFLP seizes two aircraft

over Europe. These are diverted to Dawson's Field, Jordan. Another aircraft is hijacked by the PFLP and taken to Cairo where it is blown up. A fourth hijack fails and Israeli sky marshals capture PFLP terrorist Leila Khaled.

7. September 9, 1970. The PFLP seizes yet another aircraft and it too is taken to Dawson's Field. Some three-hundred passengers are subsequently released in exchange for imprisoned Arab terrorists. This incident provokes King Hussein to force the Palestinian terrorist groups to leave Jordan.
8. May 31, 1972. The Lod Airport massacre is perpetrated by Japanese Red Army elements in a surrogate attack for the PFLP. In this attack at the Tel Aviv air terminal, twenty-six people are killed and seventy-six wounded.
9. June 27, 1976. An Air France aircraft is seized by PFLP and Baader-Meinhof terrorists and diverted to Entebbe, Uganda. After prolonged negotiations and threats by the terrorists to kill the Jewish passengers unless imprisoned Arab terrorists are released, the hijack is brought to a spectacular end by the Israeli military, who had sent in paratroops. Both the German terrorists involved are killed, as well as five members of the PFLP.
10. February 18, 1978. PFLP terrorists kill Egyptian Yusuf Sebai and then hijack a Cyprus Airways jet. The aircraft is taken to Nicosia, where an Egyptian commando operation to capture the terrorists goes awry and fifteen people die in a gunfight with the Cyprus National Guard.
11. December 6, 1984. Two American officials are killed during the hijacking of a Kuwaiti airbus by Islamic Jihad elements in Tehran. Four hijackers are arrested when the aircraft is stormed by Iranian security personnel. The perpetrators of the hijacking and murders are not prosecuted or extradited.

12. June 30, 1985. Thirty-nine Americans are released by Shi'ite terrorists at Beirut after the terrorists hijack a TWA aircraft on a flight from Athens to Rome. One American passenger is killed during a seventeen-day siege, which ends when Shi'ite Muslim prisoners held in Israel are freed.
13. November 24, 1985. An EgyptAir Boeing is seized on a flight from Athens by Abu Nidal terrorists. The aircraft is diverted to Malta where it is eventually stormed by an Egyptian commando team. The final death toll is sixty-one.
14. December 27, 1985. Abu Nidal terrorists simultaneously attack El Al ticket counters at Vienna and Rome airports. Nineteen people are killed and one-hundred-and-twelve injured.
15. April 17, 1986. El Al security personnel at Heathrow Airport, London, intercept a Palestinian terrorist-group courier who is found to be carrying a suitcase bomb. Unaware of the nature of the "contraband" she is attempting to smuggle through, the courier and her co-passengers only escape death thanks to the efforts of the El Al security staff. It is an indication of the utter callousness of the Palestinian terror groups that the courier was in this case the pregnant girlfriend of one of the terror-team members.
16. September 6, 1985. Five Arab-speaking gunmen dressed as airport security personnel storm PanAm Boeing 747 at Karachi airport, Pakistan. Demands that the aircraft be flown to Cyprus to free convicted terrorists in jail there are thwarted by the aircraft's flight crew, who escape down an emergency "ladder" as the first shots are fired. After a siege lasting some sixteen hours, Pakistani "commandos" assault the aircraft. The day's events leave more than fourteen people dead and some one hundred-and-fifty injured.

Aside from the apparent shift away from the mainstream Palestinian liberation groups as the main source of airline terrorism and a rise in actions by extremist PLO splinter groups and Shi'ite groups, at least one other fact becomes clear from the above examples. It is quite simply that regardless of previous experience, it appears that certain authorities seem unable or unwilling to implement effective countermeasures.

The "unwillingness" contention is not as fatuous as it might first appear. It costs a great deal of money and generates considerable inconvenience to *completely* secure all aspects of air travel which might be vulnerable to terrorist groups. The combination of the financial investment required and the fear of loss of revenue which could result from effective but unpopular countermeasures is sufficient to deter their implementation by all but the most threatened carriers and terminal operators. El Al, as an example, has not suffered a hijacking incident since 1970; but its rigorous attention to detail is unique, and one wonders whether similar techniques applied elsewhere would be tolerated by any but a minority of travelers.

* * *

In any case, there is an inherent flaw in all security systems, which we may loosely define as the human element. Given all the funding and popular support available, this single factor can—and indeed does—still defeat even the most advanced and effective of countermeasures. The following scenario goes some way to showing why.

> It is five-thirty in the afternoon at a large international airport. The weather is fine, and planes are arriving and departing more or less on schedule. The day has been quiet so far, and a recent investment in new technology to defeat terrorism seems to be paying off. Already the X-ray scanners through which all passengers and baggage must pass before being allowed into the departure

lounge have turned up a variety of illegal items—knives, a small handgun, several rounds of ammunition—the usual. The X-ray operators work only a "twenty minutes on, ten minutes off" shift to keep boredom from lowering their concentration levels. The system seems to be working well. If any small metal items (keys, for example) trigger the magnetometer screens, passengers are required to empty their pockets completely; the contents are then checked by guards. Most travelers accept this mild inconvenience as the price one must pay for security. A few voice their opinions to the contrary loudly, but the guards take it in stride and smile benignly.

The public-address system crackles, and a young female voice announces the imminent departure of Flight 755. Passengers stretch their legs that have stiffened due to a forty-minute wait in almost-comfortable seats, and shuffle toward the boarding area. As they leave the lounge, guards again subject them to another magnetometer screening and an explosives check. Any hand baggage carried by passengers is opened again and searched thoroughly, and two cannisters of lighter gas are confiscated from an elderly gentleman who had not seen the warning notices. Passengers and armed guards board a shuttle bus and are driven out to the waiting 737. From the perimeter of the airfield, armed military personnel maintain a watchful presence. The perimeter fence is more than thirty feet high in places, and electrified, but the military presence is constant—just in case.

The bus drives up alongside the 737, but motorized access steps will not be driven in until all passengers have claimed their waiting baggage and satisfied the security guards that all is in order. After a short delay, the signal is given, the access steps arrive, and passengers are allowed to board. The resident air-marshal guards for the journey make one last check and give the go-ahead for takeoff preparations.

Forty minutes later, the aircraft is under the control of armed hijackers, and two air marshals lie dead in the aisle. With the body of the aircraft ruptured by small-arms fire, the pilot has had to make a bumpy descent from the arranged flight-path. It makes little difference in any case, as a new destination has been demanded by the hijackers. As the aircraft sweeps westward and ground-control radar operators notice that something is wrong, the hijackers begin collecting passports from the passengers and deciding who will be first to die in the name of the cause. Back at the terminal, a maintenance operative checks his watch and glances skyward. He smiles. He has done his job well and by now his comrades should have retrieved the hidden weapons. A clever idea, he muses to himself, to make sure the toilet showed signs of use just before boarding commenced—not even those keen guards would poke around in that looking for weapons!

The human element, then, will always be the weak link in any security chain, by design or aberration, and the terrorist team with sufficient motivation can circumvent all conventional airport security measures by striking from within. It is for this reason, among others, that many authorities are now turning their attention to the employees and support personnel who have access to the aircraft during the normal course of their duties. There have also been several reports over the years of individuals employed at air terminals selling their passes and identity cards for cash, reporting them as lost or stolen. In November 1985, a reporter from a British newspaper borrowed an identity card from an employee at Heathrow Airport and walked, unquestioned, out to a waiting Concorde aircraft which he subsequently boarded. He remained in the aircraft for some fifteen minutes before concluding that he had proven the point. In this particular terminal, the going rate for "lost" cards was, apparently, £200.[6] Illegal access may also be achieved with the use of stolen uniforms or, as such thefts will nowadays cause any existing security measures to be enhanced, with the use of uniforms purchased legally from surplus stores. Even if the entire ground-staff complement of every airport in the world were beyond corruption, and assuming also that none of them ever developed an ideology-provoked desire to help some terrorist cause, there still remains the risk of one of these unimpeachable individuals being forced to comply with demands from some extremist group under threat of death or injury to a spouse or family member.

Similarly, even if stringent checks and surveillance techniques totally prevented the covert conveyance of weapons onto aircraft prior to takeoff, seizure of the plane could still be effected by a team of unarmed men. It has been known, after all, for people to kill with their bare hands. A determined terrorist squad could physically seize passengers and defy any air marshals present to shoot. Many marshals, if not all, would surely refrain, and find themselves in the unenviable position of having to hand over their own weapons. These could then be turned against them, of course. They would have to stand impotently by and watch as passengers were murdered. An innocent trouser belt, in the hands of a suitably motivated individual, becomes an effective garrotte.[7]

A FURTHER LEVEL OF AIR-SECURITY MEASURES

Aside from the obvious countermeasures of X-ray equipment, metal-sensing, and explosive sensing equipment, and armed guards and air marshals, there exists a variety of less-apparent measures which, when employed properly, serve to deter or prevent terrorist attacks to some degree. They include:

Psychological Profiles

Training airport personnel in psychological-profile recognition enables them to identify individuals whose modus operandi conforms to established parameters within which potential threats have been proven to fall. The parameters change from time to time and from area to area. For example, in 1969 thirty-five behavioral characteristics common to known hijackers were identified by a team under the direction of Dr. Evan W. Pickeral. The FAA chose not to recommend that airlines use the results, but before very long the airlines themselves did adopt the principles involved. Soon afterward, another, simpler profile was developed by Dr. David Hubbard, a psychiatrist. One of the facts upon which this profile was based was that in the United States at that time over 95 percent of hijackers had been men between eighteen and forty-five years old who had paid for one-way tickets in cash.[8] Thus it was sensible to conclude that women purchasing round-trip tickets on credit cards, for example, posed less of a threat. A current profile would take into account other factors, including religious denomination and prior travel status. The hijacker of today, in contrast to his Sixties counterpart, is more likely to travel first class, pay with credit cards, and generally give the impression of being a well-heeled businessman.[9] (If he is a PLO operative, of course, he probably *is* a well-heeled businessman.)

Use of the 16PF test may also identify individuals concealing dangerous personality defects. This is but one of a number of related tests that may be used to determine both the general mental condition of an individual and his or her likely reactions in a given situation.

In the context of terrorism, an ability to obtain such an indication—even if it is only of a general nature—can be of great help in denying the terrorist operative access to potential targets. Several large companies already use this type of test when assessing the suitability of potential directors or other personnel who are to be employed in important capacities. While the results of such tests are often dismissed as being applicable only to the obviously disturbed or "abnormal," this is not the case. No one would suggest that every terrorist could be identified on the strength of test results alone—to do that would first require a concrete definition of "terrorist," and this (as we have seen) is unobtainable—but as part of an overall picture, the importance of these tests cannot be overlooked. An inclination toward violence, for example, can be determined by the use of such tests. If an individual is found to possess this trait in greater or lesser measure than the next fellow, this might suggest something about what situations are suitable for him.

An important aspect of such tests is their built-in "validity scales." These help the examiner assess how honestly and carefully the candidate has answered the questions. It is not possible to "lie" or "cheat" on the tests, as there is no correct or incorrect set of answers. All answers indicate *some* quality of the subject. For the most part, these tests are multiple-choice types, and can consequently be completed in a reasonably short time. Initial "rough" assessment can be achieved with use of an answer matrix; thus an unskilled person is able to give and score the test. If some aspect of the subject's response implies an unstable or dangerous personality, the person administering the test can at once call for more qualified personnel. The future may see such tests being part of applying for a visa for entry into terrorist-threatened countries.

"Watchers"

Known by various names in different parts of the world, "watchers" are individuals with photographic memories provided by security or intelligence agencies. Their task is simply to watch passengers and ground staff and try to recognize one of the many faces they have studied in "wanted" or "suspect" lists. Capable of spotting one face among thousands, these operatives frequently concentrate on recognizing any of half a dozen especially wanted fugitives according to a list determined on a day-to-day or week-to-week basis.

Electronic Surveillance

Located at strategic points around air terminals, cameras–some obvious, some hidden–are linked to monitors which are watched constantly for signs of potential danger. In some countries (Sweden being one), hidden still cameras are installed above airport immigration-desk booths. When the traveler presents his documents for examination, the immigration officer, if he feels further checks are in order or if a request has been made by some authority for some special surveillance, will casually maneuver the passport, for example, into a central position on the desk and fire the overhead camera with a footswitch. The traveler remains unaware that a photograph has been taken. Voice recorders may also be found in similar situations. Voice prints thus obtained are checked against existing records and then stored for future reference on computer.

If immediate reaction is not required, visual surveillance may be maintained with film, as opposed to video, cameras. Ticket purchase points are commonly monitored in this fashion. Some of the current 16mm equipment in use takes more than 8,000 frames of film with a single loading–one picture every 18 seconds for forty hours. Each frame is automatically given a date and time for future reference. It is probable that in the future, aircraft will also carry electronic surveillance systems. These would be triggered only when an irreversible panic button were thrown by a member of the crew. Current technology suggests that a miniature television camera and transmitter could send a signal to ranges of around one hundred miles or so from an aircraft flying at, say, 30,000 feet. The signals—visual and audio—would be received by towers and reaction forces. Precise knowledge of hijacker numbers, temperament, and intentions, as well as the positioning of hostages, is of inestimable value to groups planning a rescue assault.

No-Panic Codes

These are simply prearranged phrases which may be announced over public-address systems to alert all security personnel and other staff to an emergency situation without alarming passengers and terminal visitors. "Telephone call for Mr. Green, please use the yellow phone" is a typical example. In such an instance, there would be no yellow phone, but the only people aware of this would be airport staff. Sometimes the codes are "graded," enabling selected personnel to react as the situation demands. In many cases there exists a "full alert" code, upon receipt of which the relevant staff puts into effect a prearranged emergency plan. This usually consists of subtly redirecting passengers away from the danger area. Many a passenger has found himself, at the behest of some smiling official, traveling a circuitous route back to whence he started within an airport terminal, happily oblivious that a bomb threat has been made against the building.

What to Do If You're on a Hijacked Airplane

As we have seen, despite all efforts to the contrary, terrorist attacks of varying natures will, from time to time, prove successful. There is very little that the traveler can do if such an attack is made, say, with surface-to-air missiles. The best that can be said about such incidents is that if they *are* successful, there is every chance that the passenger will never know anything about it. The same might be said of in-flight bomb explosions. An incredible exception to this is the case of a Yugoslavian air stewardess who, in 1972, survived a thirty-three-thousand-foot fall to earth in the wreckage of an aircraft ripped apart in mid-air by a Croatian bomb.

Certain sensible precautions can be taken, however, by all but the traveler who—for reasons beyond his control—must travel from A to B at a certain time, regardless of risk. Careful selection of the carrier is the first consideration, with a view to selecting the most security conscious. Restrictions on the type of hand baggage which may be taken on-board, a search of the aircraft before takeoff, luggage claims on the ramp, etc., all indicate a lower risk value—other things being equal—than that posed by carriers whose sole concern is a rapid turnaround. The traveler is within his rights to ask what precautions are in effect. Many professional agencies in fact suggest that this be done, primarily because any indication that passengers are security conscious will be fed back to a carrier's senior personnel and could well prove instrumental in bringing about greater attention to relevant details. No one would expect that sensitive security details will be proffered by check-in staff—even if they are aware of them—but the girl who smiles and says "Excuse me?" when asked what antihijack precautions are in force is obviously a representative of a carrier whose policy toward security is dubious. Air terminals might also be selected on a security basis. Those at which metal-detection screens are tuned down so as not to trigger on "insignificant" items are obviously less secure than those at which even a bunch of keys sets the lights flashing. Indeed, if a bunch of keys does not trigger the alarm, then neither will a small "micro-pistol" of the same metal content. Tuning down these screens is very common practice at many airports.[10]

Should the traveler find himself in a hijack situation, the safest reaction technique will be simply to stay calm, avoid direct eye contact with the perpetrators, volunteer no comment or opinion unless it is demanded, and comply with any instructions immediately. At all costs, avoid provoking a reaction by moving suddenly or trying any actual "heroics." Do not reach into pockets for cigarettes. If security guards are present, there is a more-than-even chance that an exchange of gunfire will take place. Should this occur, stay down behind seats and resist any temptation to crawl or run to a "safer" part of the aircraft. One is as likely to run *into* gunfire in such situations as away from it. Only move once again when an intelligible command is heard indicating beyond doubt that the immediate danger is over. It may be that the guards have contained the terrorists, or killed them, or vice versa.

It will become apparent before too long precisely what the terrorists are seeking to achieve by their actions. A fanatical religious group may immediately begin killing all members of certain "enemy" denominations. A less selective group may choose victims at random or on the basis of symbolic value. They might choose, for example, military personnel or persons wearing expensive jewelry. The death order selected by hijackers of the EgyptAir Boeing in 1985 was, according to details provided by several of the hostages themselves: First in line, two Israeli girls; then three Americans; then Australians, Canadians, and West Europeans. Passports were taken from passengers in this instance and used to determine the various nationalities. They were then reseated accordingly. In situations involving less thorough perpetrators, an opportunity may present itself to adopt the role of a less threatened category. An American, for example, may find it prudent to claim that he is Canadian, Australian, or even British. In an international travel situation, passports will usually be readily available—either carried on the person or in nearby hand baggage. If, however, the passport were in baggage stowed in the cargo hold, it would be harder for the terrorist to confirm or refute a passenger's nationality status! In a ship hijacking, there is a far greater chance of successfully claiming a different nationality, as passports are frequently left in cabins. In either case, a degree of acting ability is called for. It is useful to note that this skill saved the life of Patrick Scott-Baker, an American, shot by terrorists during the Malta hijacking. Pushed to the floor and shot in the neck by one of the terrorists, Scott-Baker feigned death and was thrown down the steps of the aircraft on to the field, where he lay until collected by a medical team. The medical team, like the hijackers, thought they were dealing with a corpse.[11]

NOTES

1. J. Bowyer Bell, *A Time of Terror* (New York: Basic Books, 1978), p. 59.

2. Ibid., p. 60.

3. International Air Transport Association figures.

4. Walter Laqueur, *Terrorism* (Weidenfield and Nicolson, 1977), p. 108.

5. Compiled from International Air Transport Association figures and other sources.

6. This example of ineffective security measures at British air terminals was not unique. In the same month Mr. Edwin Buckhalter, a member of the British air passengers' watchdog group, The Air Transport Users Committee, walked onto a Quantas airline Boeing 747 at Heathrow while he was waiting for another flight. He was able to look around for some time without being challenged.

7. As the massacres at Rome and Vienna airports in November 1985 illustrated, even when security screening systems preclude the successful conveyance of terrorist weaponry into embarking areas and onto planes, the precheck-in lounge area can still be attacked with frightening effect. These attacks–perpetrated by the Libyan-supported Al Fatah Revolutionary Council, an Abu Nidal group–provoked the deployment of police

carrying automatic weapons at some British air terminals for the first time. While this will possible deter some terrorist factions, one can see clearly from the Rome and Vienna incidents that the only sure way to deny terrorists access to an easy kill is by searching *all* passengers as they enter the building. To this end, we may in the future see X-ray equipment and physical searches at terminal entrances. Baggage is thus checked before travelers enter the terminal building at all. This will effectively push back the "frontier," which currently exists at the check-in desks. Security at the check-in desks has been working quite well. The same measures could be expected to be effective, then, at the point of first entry as well. Despite frequent comments to the contrary by persons whom one can only assume have a vested interest in the maintenance of the existing system, I cannot believe that an air terminal entry procedure which requires the traveler to deposit all except carry-on baggage on a conveyor (via which the baggage would travel through a screening system) before entering the building proper and to submit both himself and any remaining hand baggage to a physical search at the same point, would be overly expensive to introduce, either in terms of hard cash or passenger inconvenience. Such a technique, however, in combination with an improvised passenger segregation system in the check-in areas proper, would greatly reduce the number of available target passengers for terrorist attack. There are, of course, many other possible countermeasures, and while none of them can *completely* preclude a terrorist assault of some type, their introduction could serve to force the would-be terrorist aggressor to adopt methods which would be so extreme or complex as to render them futile.

8. J. Bowyer Bell, p. 140.

9. One of several comments attributed to United States security personnel in an article published in Birmingham, England's *Daily News,* 26 November 1985.

10. Author's personal experience at several minor air terminals in the United States and Europe. The X-ray viewing systems through which all baggage should pass, like the metal-detecting units, can be defeated.

In November 1985, various sources reported that special cases of the Samsonite type, which had been adapted to defeat the X-ray scanners at airports, were being used by Shi'ite Muslim terrorists. The technique became widely known around October 1985, when two Arabs were arrested at Rome Airport carrying a suitcase lined with explosive material. The two basic ways of defeating such equipment are to alter the metal components in a device to resemble an innocent item, or to have a second party carry part of the device and then reassemble it on the aircraft. Sophisticated suitcase bombs have detonators that are not connected to the explosive by wires (which, unless disguised or camouflaged among other case contents, could be spotted by an alert scanner operator) but are built into, for example, a pocket calculator. The calculator, quite legitimately, carries enough circuitry and power to activate a small on-board primary charge. The proximity of this calculator-detonator to the main explosive charge hidden in the case is such that the whole bomb will detonate. Certain types of thin, plastic explosives are not visible to X-ray scanners, and thus the explosive may be a thin layer covering the entire bottom of a false-bottom case.

Other bomb cases have defeated detection thanks to the ingenuity of their designers. The "Ibrahim" case bombs, for example, had detonators carefully placed behind the metal case locks, thereby hiding them from the scanner rays. Increased and *proper* use of explosive sniffers will lessen the chance of similar devices passing unnoticed.

There are also designs available for pen guns that can be carried quite openly in a pocket without attracting suspicion save from the most skilled and experienced of security personnel. A thorough physical search is required to determine their presence, let alone their true purpose, and thus the number of airports at which, at this time, they would be detected are very few indeed. Other items of varying shapes and sizes may be covertly taken onto aircraft by individuals having referred first to such publications as *Duty Free, Sneak It Through,* and *How to Hide Anything.* These books (by Michael Connor) are available from Paladin Press, Boulder, Colorado.

11. *London Times,* 25 November 1985.

9

Communications

The potential terrorist targets which fall into this category warrant a chapter in their own right by virtue of the fact that the past few years have seen a quantum leap forward in communications technology: satellites, microwaves, frequency-hopping radio, fiber-optics—the list goes on and on. A side effect of these developments, however, is that society has come to depend on this technology for its daily communication and thus is as vulnerable as the technology is effective—and it is very effective indeed.

TELEPHONES

A successful attack against the telephone system is made more probable by the ease with which many of the new landline links may be destroyed. Fiber-optic lines are currently being used to replace the traditional multicore cable; and, while this makes for increased information transmission, it also means that for a given amount of effort the terrorist can effect more disruption. As part of a low-profile assault, the terrorist would need only to cut through bundles of flexible plastic or fiberglass, or contaminate the same with an organic solvent to which the material is sensitive. This presents far less of a problem than sawing or hacking through heavy metal cables. The fiber-optic material is screened with a protective cover, of course, to withstand the rigors of underground burial, but the structure is overall far more delicate. A small bottle of acid—easily concealed and transported—would prove even more effective than organic solvents. Accessing the lines via any of the easily opened inspection and maintenance covers, which pepper every city, the terrorist could simply pour the acid over a small area of the line. He could be confident that within minutes it would permeate the outer coverings and begin to eat away at the fibers. Repair of such damage would require far more effort and time than a repair to conventional cabling. In addition, such a repair could not be made by an unskilled worker, as is possible with conventional cabling (which can be repaired simply by twisting broken wire ends back together or by patching in extra lengths).

* * *

Even an opportunist assault on an isolated telephone circuit might generate effects beyond initial expectation:

> A political meeting in a volatile area of a big city has provoked an angry reaction from some of the audience. Tempers flare and fighting breaks out. Ejected from the building, the antagonists continue their dispute in the street. Seeing the potential in this situation, a terrorist sympathizer working nearby on a street-repair crew lifts an inspection cover and drives a pick into the cables below. Since they are of optical fiber, there is no current present, and therefore no electrical flash. The fighting continues across the street, and the local criminal element soon gathers to witness what seems to be an amusing interlude to an otherwise boring afternoon. It is only a short while before this casual interest turns into aggressive involvement.
>
> Local residents and workers, concerned that the

situation is deteriorating rapidly, try to telephone the police but find that the lines are dead. Autocall alarm systems, linked into the phone system, are now useless as well, and news of this soon spreads to the still-growing crowd, many of whom are not slow to take advantage. As they have received no complaints from the area, the police remain oblivious to the situation until a routine patrol arrives on the scene some time later. By this stage, however, stores have been looted, people seriously injured, and the incident is beyond immediate containment. Over the next few days, the city is plagued by similar incidents as imitators–inspired by press reports of the affair–set about disabling the phone lines in other areas.

* * *

Rather than destroying sections of telephone system, a terrorist group may choose to maintain a very low profile and tap into the network instead. Sensitive information secured in this manner might be used in a variety of ways. Leaking confidential details, for example, pertaining to a defense contract, would seriously undermine the confidence of shareholders in the company concerned, as well as cast doubt on the ability of government and security agencies to keep official secrets secret. The precise nature of the information need not be particularly outstanding. A capability having been demonstrated, many people would accept that "it might not have been important this time, but what about the next?" Similarly, if, via the use of telephone taps and the like, the terrorist group were able to determine precisely what type of reaction it could expect from government agencies faced with certain demands and threats, the group itself would be better placed to ensure that any such demands they made fell just short of being totally unacceptable. They would be fairly certain, in other words, what they could and could not get away with in any subsequent negotiations.

MICROWAVE DISHES

Microwave dishes are a familiar sight nowadays atop towers or roof-mounted supports. By design, this type of antenna is very directional and needs accurate alignment if it is to prove effective. It is most often used as a link across line-of-sight terrain as any objects in between the dishes cause serious attenuation or complete loss of signal. Some telephone networks use radio frequencies suitable for transmission via this type of antenna, as do many private companies and the military. In the telephone context, a combination of landline and microwave dish is common. Damage to or destruction of even a single dish used in this application can cause the loss of literally millions of national and international calls. If the network is used by broadcast radio stations as well, as is often the case, their transmissions would also be lost.

Because these dishes must be mounted clear of surrounding obstacles, they are frequently found in the middle of deserted fields or on the tops of very tall buildings. Only when the dish is mounted on top of a building used by the transmitting company for other purposes are security measures of any significance likely to be encountered. For the most part, a token fence or warning sign is all that exists to deter "interested" individuals.

A few rounds of well-aimed small-caliber rifle fire are all that would be needed to completely cripple such dishes. Or, if close access were possible, a few smacks with a hammer. Simply denting in the central (exposed) waveguide causes massive problems in transmission and reception. As the runup to more serious attacks or as part of a long-term destabilization program, these units could be primary targets.

RADIO-FREQUENCY INTERFERENCE (RFI)

Destruction of microwave antenna dishes is, as we

have seen, a cheap and easy way to disrupt communications. Destruction or damage to them, however, can easily be prevented by simply posting guards nearby. The terrorist, then, may choose to jam a communication network rather than damage a specific physical aspect.

The benefit to the terrorist of using such a method is that authorities will be initially unsure who or what is generating the interference and with what purpose. Also, as distinct from physical sabotage, the jamming will be almost impossible to prevent. Local police frequencies are a highly probable target in peacetime, although NATO frequencies and those of related agencies are also at high risk. Determining what frequencies are in use by a given sender is a simple matter of listening in to a wide-band, multi-mode scanner. The search may be hastened by the purchase of various lists—regularly advertised in radio hobby magazines—which give explicit details on who uses what part of the radio spectrum, why, when, and how. Moves are afoot in some countries to restrict the sale of both scanner receivers and frequency lists, but even if such measures were implemented they would achieve little beyond deterring the truly casual listener.

What technology is required to seriously interfere with radio communications depends to some extent on the type of system targeted; but whatever may be required is readily available from a variety of sources. Several American publications regularly carry small advertisements of offers to build radio transmitters to specifications submitted by the purchaser. While to do so is illegal unless the proposed user is licensed by the FCC, the authorities have better things to do with their time than track down essentially harmless "pirates." The technically qualified terrorist—and this qualification need not extend much beyond amateur radio standards—could build his own small, but powerful, transmitters for a few dollars by utilizing modern components which, in solid-state, "chip" form, replicate the functions of what just a few years ago had to be accomplished with dozens of separate, larger components.

By placing the transmitter(s) strategically, interference may be generated on a general or specific level. If interference with mobile police communications is desired, for example, a few field tests with his own receiver would allow the terrorist to determine at what points around the target area the strength of the target transmitter dropped to easily defeatable levels. In cities, the presence of large buildings, steel and concrete structures, and power lines all serve to cause pockets of attenuation which are effective no-go areas for radio communication on certain frequencies. Similarly, at the extremes of the transmitters' range—again determined by field tests—reception will fall off or end abruptly. By placing transmitters near to already poor reception areas, these effects can be increased; by placing more within normally good reception areas, further no-communication points can be created. A vehicle ambushed at such points would be unable to call for assistance. Thus, as the number of such locations increases, so do the risks to radio-linked personnel.

Another way of using small battery-powered transmitters, which can (indeed, often does) prove extremely disruptive, is the placement of such devices close to transmitters used for police or military communications. For ease of access, the terrorist could target remote relay (repeater) stations. At close range, the target transmitter would suffer extreme interference and, depending on the frequency of the signal and the mode (FM, AM, SSB, ACSB, etc.), may retransmit the interference to other stations tuned to its signal. Some relay stations are triggered simply by the arrival of the incoming signal. In such cases, a simple timer device coupled to the jammer would keep such stations tied-up indefinitely. Other relays require that the incoming signal carry an additional coded signal before they "open." These may be single tone bursts, multi-tones, or inaudible coded pulses. All of these are receivable and replicable.

A light-activated switch, available cheaply from electronic stores, could be connected to the jamming transmitter in such a manner as to render it operative only at nightfall. This would seriously hamper the efforts of any search team detailed to locate the source of the interference, as it would only be able to search during hours of darkness. This technique was used in the late 1970s by various anti-NATO factions active in West Germany.[1]

FREQUENCY-HOPPING RADIO

Modern military communication links employ satellite and frequency-hopping equipment which, though efficient and reliable under normal circumstances, is nowhere near as "interception proof" as many people might believe. As the name suggests, frequency-hopping radio systems change frequency constantly on a random or pre-programmed basis, thereby defeating the efforts of an interceptor to follow the passage of information. Also, since the number of possible frequencies that might be used at any one time is enormous, conventional wide-spectrum jamming is generally not effective. A piece of equipment called the Bragg Cell,[2] however, overcomes the problem.

Without becoming overly technical, we can say that the unit utilizes acoustic energy generated by an incoming signal to deflect or modulate a laser beam passing through a lithium niobiate crystal. The angle of deflection is directly proportional to the frequency of the signal. Thus it is possible to determine that frequency with associated electronic devices. The unit is a quite recent development, but its sale is not subject to any governmental restrictions. A qualified radio engineer would be able to design and build a complete system for interception or–linking two such systems–jamming purposes at a cost disproportionate in the extreme to its worth for a terrorist campaign. The erroneous belief that a force's communications network is beyond interception or disruption has obvious dangers, and it may be the technical terrorist rather than the invading paratrooper who ultimately proves the point.

Radio-frequency interception techniques also lend themselves well to aircraft hijack/attack scenarios. Many of today's aircraft sport highly sophisticated, computerized flight control and navigation systems, and these may be interfered with deliberately with little effort. An electronics package no bigger than a Sony Walkman cassette player and capable of wreaking havoc with flight instruments could easily be taken on-board an aircraft by a terrorist and switched on during the flight—with potentially disastrous consequences. To negate the risk of being overpowered by cabin staff (who might then disable the device), the terrorists can find an unwitting accomplice who would be paid to "smuggle" some item for them. The actual "contraband" would be a timer-controlled flight deck jammer, set to turn on in mid-flight. Thus the terrorist group might successfully destroy the aircraft and its passengers with far greater ease than would be the case if explosives were employed.

COMPUTERS

It would be an understatement to say that the use of computers in both civil and military applications is widespread. An oft-overlooked aspect of this, however, is that many of the larger support-and-control computer systems have been built up cumulatively. This has the consequence that no one really knows any more *exactly* what the system is capable of nor what the original parameters of its program were. Its users can take information out and add information as the need arises, but detailed analysis of the system and identification of the original source of particular data is often not possible. A large amount of information output from such systems is, therefore, taken for granted as accurate and genuine without any attempt at cross-checking. Indeed, to resort to such cross-checking would defeat the whole purpose of computers in the first place. This effectively means that the terrorist, armed with only basic knowledge and some elementary pieces of equipment, may enter many computer systems and withdraw, alter, or add to the information therein with a very low probability of detection.

There are various ways in which computers may be accessed by unauthorized persons. The classic telephone and modem (modulator/demodulator) technique favored by hackers may still be used in a number of circumstances, although the instances of illegal system entry by this means have been so numerous that an entire cottage industry revolving around telephone-line protection has sprung up. Devices for encoding/encrypting and scrambling information passing down landlines are now available in a variety of forms. Surprisingly, however, those agencies which would seem in an ideal position to defeat attempts at illegal phone-and-modem access frequently appear unable or unwilling to do so. Take, for example, the case of two sixteen-year-olds from Nevada who, appalled at their phone bills, hacked into the telephone company's central billing computer and erased their own records. A four-month investigation by the company did eventually track down the youngsters, and in 1985 they were charged with attempting to defraud Sierra Telecom of approximately eight thousand dollars.[3] That this can happen to a company which, one suspects, has access to the latest in countermeasures says a good deal. Organized crime has also not been slow to take advantage of the inherent weaknesses in computer systems. In one interesting case, two hundred boxcars were written off a railway company's inventory by operatives who accessed its main stock computer. What would organized crime want with 200 boxcars? They promptly leased them back to the original owners.[4]

In detail, the standard technique referred to here involves linking an external computer to the target computer via the telephone system. This is achieved using a modem, of which there are two basic types. The first connects directly to the input/output port of the penetrator's computer, bypassing the telephone handset completely. The second type–often called an acoustic coupler–does connect via the handset and "codes" and "decodes" the audio signal. The penetrator will need to know the language understood by the target computer–there are only a few possibilities, information about which is readily available–as well as the phone number at which it can be reached and any passwords or access codes in use at the time.

Passwords are simply words or sequences of words and/or numbers which must be input to the computer before it permits deeper operator access. It is not hard for the penetrator to discover these passwords. A terrorist may secure employment within the target company or within a company which has access to the target computer and obtain the necessary information from legitimate users by stealth or bribery. Passwords and access codes are frequently left unprotected in drawers or filing cabinets, or even pinned to notice boards or taped to on-site terminals. Even if passwords are changed daily, someone will have to notify users of the current code, and in such cases the potential exists for even an office helper to secure the information. Alternatives include subtle questioning of maintenance or installation personnel, many of whom will have "shortcut" or "master" access codes to facilitate speed of repair. If these techniques cannot be used, the terrorist penetrator may simply tap the phone lines going into the target computer building and record all the data passing down them. This will include, of course, a variety of access codes pertaining to different users and applications.

It is also possible to allow the remote computer to try to determine the access code itself by programming it with complex algorithms. Information databases even exist, the operators of which will sell lists of the "top ten" most popular "log-on" and access codes.

A more recent development known as "Tempest" involves tuning in with suitable equipment to the radio frequency signals given off by the computer visual display unit (VDU) or some other piece of electronic data-processing equipment. These signals carry the same information that is being displayed on the screen which, in many instances, will include the passwords or access codes entered during log-on. Equipment is commonly installed in a van or camper which the penetrator parks across the street from the target computer building. An antenna on the roof of the vehicle picks up the signals which are then fed into the decoding equipment. A real-time copy image of any information currently being displayed on the VDU is then resolved onto another screen in the vehicle, where it is recorded for future analysis.[5]

Access to many systems will present few difficulties to the terrorist, then. But what is he likely to do once "inside"? The possibilities are, in fact, considerable. The nationalist/separatist group might access the local police or military computer and extract the names of spies and infiltrators, whom they could then target or feed false information. The group requiring certain materials—explosives, radio-control equipment, etc.—might access the order facility of a supplier's computer and arrange for items to be delivered to a location in which an ambush or hijack can be made. The establishment of a fictitious company is also a possibility, and this might be done with a view to ordering and paying for items electronically which would otherwise be beyond the group's reach. Bacteria samples, for example, are available on the open market but only to bona fide companies or research or teaching establishments. Few, if any, of these suppliers will check to see if a computer-placed order is from a company which has been around for a year or a week. And very often the whole process of ordering, shipping, and invoicing is done automatically by computer.

Another possibility is to access intelligence-agency databases and remove the names of wanted persons or to alter important details pertaining to those persons. False and misleading information about politicians or military personnel may be added to a database. When the database is next accessed by operatives, the false data will be accepted as valid and generate serious resource wastage as surveillance and investigative projects are established to confirm or refute implications drawn from the information. Many such intelligence databases are shared by different governments. A computer in Berlin, for example, may be simply accessed by police agents in New York by a telephone. An interesting example of how information input by one authority is taken as factual by representatives of another is to be found in the case of a British female film director working for Michael Barratt. She was refused security clearance to direct a film. Subsequent inquiries into the grounds for this refusal revealed that, in a visit abroad with her husband, he had been mistakenly identified as a terrorist whom, it was claimed, he resembles. The unconfirmed information was passed to British police, who entered it away on their computer. The malicious terrorist variation of this might be that some prominent government minister had been seen dining with a known terrorist-group leader.

A typical international security/police computer exists in Wiesbaden, West Germany, and is known affectionately as "Kommissar." It contains information about more than ten million known and suspected terrorists, including their photographs and those of their friends and relatives, their fingerprints, voiceprints, dental records, and a variety of other information. This computer was consulted during the search for kidnapped Italian Christian Democratic Party leader Aldo Moro in 1978. He was eventually murdered by his captors—elements of the Red Brigade—when the Italian government refused to negotiate with them.[6] To imagine that any authority has the ability to cross-check and verify information relating to ten million people, even if they chose to, is foolish. The terrorist, then, might well consider the computer to be a valuable and risk-free target.

There are countermeasures against illegal computer access, and some of them we have already examined. Electronic keys are another technique which some agencies use. These resemble the credit card-type of "key" which has the "combination" encoded magnetically upon its side or back. These can be duplicated, however, by using a device known as an electronic pantograph; or, if the key is of a simple design, a normal electric iron. In the case of the former, complex electronic equipment decodes the information on the card, facilitating its replication. The iron is simply used to attach a new magnetic strip.

Encryption is by far the most effective means of preventing unauthorized access. It involves encoding and decoding the data using algorithms and a special, unique key. As long as the key is known only to the sender and recipient, the information remains secure even if the algorithms become known. Anyone intercepting data encrypted in this fashion receives only garbage, and the computer power needed to break the code down is enormous, beyond all but the largest and most modern of machines. It is interesting to note that the U.S. National Security Agency (NSA) has set a standard of seven-digit coding which it claims is unbreakable.[7] In fact, the NSA's own equipment can unscramble data thus encoded, but not data encoded eight times. This implies that the NSA has an understandable desire to retain the ability to unscramble every other organization's encrypted data.

SATELLITES

At an average distance from earth of some 22,300

miles, one might expect that communication satellites were safe from the terrorist's attentions. This is not the case. While it is unlikely that a private sector space shuttle capability will be of any serious interest to a terror group (although the larger of such groups certainly have the funding for such a project), terrorists will undoubtedly soon take heed of the potential for remote attack so ably demonstrated by the likes of "Captain Midnight." The good Captain is an American electronics buff whose most famous exploit to date was the jamming of an HBO (Home Box Office) company feature film, *Falcon and the Snowman.* The satellite-transmitted picture vanished for around five minutes, during which time it was replaced with a test pattern and the words "Good evening from Captain Midnight. $12.95 a month? No way. Showtime/Movie Channel beware."

The "$12.95 a month, no way" comment was a reference to the price charged per month by HBO for a decoder which viewers need to watch the scrambled satellite pictures. Our pirate Captain was warning other satellite operators of what could happen if they too chose to scramble programs.

HBO engineers increased the power of the uplink—the signal from earth to the satellite—but were unsure whether they had overridden the Captain or if he had voluntarily switched off after making his point. The company had received threats of program interruption prior to this event, but had considered the power needed to "capture" the satellite's on-board receiver/transmitter (the Transponder) to be beyond the reach of "amateurs."

HBO technicians and the Federal Communications Commission (FCC) investigators expressed a belief that the hijack, which they dubbed an act of "video terrorism," would have required a power output from the pirate station of around four kilowatts and an antenna dish the size of at least five meters in diameter.

A lesser publicized incident occurred in Britain when

the "Sky Channel" was prevented from getting its signal on the Eutelsat satellite, and thence out across Europe, by a pirate station beaming up a rival signal. The perpetrator(s) of this incident was never identified. The authorities do not like to admit that an interloper operating in short bursts cannot be located. The technology for serious interference is not overly expensive and is well within the grasp of private individuals, let alone sponsored terror groups.

Using the same principles–the transmission of a signal which overrides the legitimate satellite uplink–a terror group could not only jam the earthbound signals from a satellite, perhaps replacing the legitimate program with a propaganda message or threat, but could, with inside knowledge, turn the satellite off or alter its position in space. A transmitting dish looks like a receiving dish and thus the terrorist could openly install the unit in a backyard without fear of attracting unwanted attention. The transmitting equipment proper would, of course, be hidden indoors.

The inside knowledge required by the group or individual would be the specific signal codes which the satellite could "understand" and react to. This information could be secured by trial and error, by subtle questioning of company employees, by infiltrating the company, or by outright theft. It is even possible that the techno-terrorist could wait until a new satellite were launched and then monitor the command signals emanating from its earth control station. These recorded signals could then be "edited" to create a new sequence of commands.

NOTES

1. Conversations with British military personnel who served in West Germany during that period.

2. Conversation with a British electronics engineer.

3. *Computing Age,* December 1985.

4. Ibid.

5. Techniques acquired by author during operations on behalf of British counter-surveillance and security agency.

6. The body of Aldo Moro was found on 10 May, 1978 in the back of a car in the Via Caetani, Rome. He had been killed with eleven bullets, fired into the body at close range.

7. Various press statements from NSA representatives, 1985.

10

Hostages and Sieges

While the practice of hostage-taking by terrorist groups is not to be condoned or encouraged, there is much to be said for the belief that such actions are infinitely preferable to outright murder. At least in the case of hostage-taking there exists some hope for a bloodless conclusion. It has also to be admitted that the hostage/siege situation is even less likely to be prevented in the future than are bombings and shootings. This is simply because, while it takes real weapons and intent to perpetrate an aggressive attack, hostages can be (indeed have been) taken on the strength of a bluff.

The hijackers of TWA Flight 355 from New York to Chicago on September 10, 1976, maintained control of the passengers and crew by threatening to detonate "explosives" that were attached to their persons. Wires and switches were in evidence, and so was what appeared to be plastique. Having achieved their aim, which, in essence, was the publication of a manifesto concerning Croatian self-determination, the hijackers ripped apart the "bombs" and distributed the "explosives" among the passengers as a souvenir of the event. The explosives, in fact, were nothing more than clay.[1] The authorities at the airport were not confident enough in their magnetometer screening system to conclude that no bombs could have been smuggled onboard, and since a genuine device *had* been left by the hijackers in the airport itself as a warning, they had no choice but to concede to demands.

REASONS FOR HOSTAGE-TAKING

There are various reasons why a terrorist group takes hostages. It may be that they intend to demand a ransom—which might be cash, the release of prisoners, or some other concession—or they may be acting on instruction from a higher authority who is paying them, in effect, to perform a piece of theatre for the benefit of the media. In this latter case, the terrorists may or may not believe that they will succeed in escaping from the scene. Where they *do* consider an escape possible, it will not always follow that their sponsors believe so.

Hostages may also be taken as a matter of necessity or prudence. For example, the IRA often requires a specific location from which to mount a sniper attack or from which to detonate an explosion. Where the only suitable and accessible location is a private house, the perpetrators will forcibly enter the property and hold the occupier hostage until the attack is over. Similarly, if a terrorist group is intercepted in the middle of some operation, it will seize any bystanders as an insurance policy against arrest or assault. Demands issued under such circumstances are likely to be related directly to escape, i.e., transportation and money.

Police reactions to hostage situations have changed dramatically over the last decade or so. Up until 1972, the majority of incidents were still met with brute force or a stubborn refusal to negotiate, but in that year New York Police Commissioner Patrick Murphy initiated a specialist hostage reaction program, which would prove to be the first of many. One Harvey Schlossberg, a patrolman with a Ph.D. in psychology, was assigned to establish applicable guidelines and produce a training syllabus. Avoiding complex jargon, Schlossberg presented a case for calm, patience, and reasoned negotiation, and a short while later the Detective Bureau

Hostage Negotiation Team was born.[2] The team was not established specifically to deal with terrorist threats, but the suitability of the techniques for use in such situations soon became apparent.

In almost all parts of the world now, a hostage/siege situation will be met with a combined response: the negotiation team and the assault/rescue team. This latter group maintains a very low profile until it is established beyond reasonable doubt that there is nothing further to be gained by continuing with negotiation.

Once communication has been established with the hostage-takers, it will be made clear by the authorities that, although there can be no hope of escape, no harm will befall them if they release the hostages unharmed. The demands of the hostage-takers will be considered at this stage; if they are realistic and acceptable, they will—in most instances—be conceded. Nothing will ever be given, however, without some reciprocal gesture—the release of old or sick hostages, pregnant women, and so on. The nature of the demand issued by hostage-takers will often be a determining factor in precisely how the authorities react. In Los Angeles, in January 1977, twenty-one-year-old Dolpin Lain seized a hostage, and from the roof of the United California Bank building demanded attention be given to his antismoking campaign. In response, the *Los Angeles Times* printed an interview called "Stop Smoking: The Media Got His Message." Lain's father, it transpired, had died of cancer.[3] Some would consider his actions those of a madman, but it is obvious that they had the desired effect. In this instance, the demands were reasonable, easily met—indeed, the action achieved his aims. Lain was really only using a terrorist technique as a means to an end. He had absolutely nothing to gain by killing his hostage, and, although hostages have been killed for no reason other than to add emphasis to "the message," in this instance the very nature of the demands indicated a genuine concern for life. His intent was to stop people from dying unnecessarily and he was, therefore, extremely unlikely to perpetrate a murder.

Vague or irrational demands, or demands which are obviously the result of some mental aberration, give serious cause for concern, as the behavior of the hostage-taker is almost impossible to predict. Many of the Baader-Meinhof kidnappings during the 1970s were perpetrated with a view to securing the release of "political" prisoners. Frequently, the authorities complied with demands, and the hostages were subsequently released. Such incidents are clear-cut (relatively speaking). If the prisoners are released and the terrorists do *not* keep their part of the bargain, they have destroyed any hope of using the technique successfully in the future. Aware of this important fact, the group has a strong motivation to keep the bargains it has made. Compare this type of scenario, however, with the case of Cory C. Moore, an ex-Marine who, having taken hostage police captain Leo M. Keglovic in Cleveland, stipulated among other demands that all white people must leave the planet. Fortunately, after two days of negotiation and a phone call from President Carter, the siege was peacefully ended.[4]

If the deranged or disturbed present reaction problems in such situations, the religiously motivated individual or group poses the greatest threat. Such individuals tend to feel that, having been guaranteed a place in their heaven, the earthly fate that befalls them matters little. Most recently, it has been the religious groups whose attitude and behavior has most shaken the established principles of siege negotiation.

THE CAPTOR/CAPTIVE BOND

The first few minutes of a hostage-taking incident are the most dangerous. Both hostages and their captors are as tense as they are likely to be throughout the ordeal, and either can react unexpectedly and violently. Once this initial stage is over, however, things tend to settle somewhat and the situation becomes less volatile. A waiting game starts in which police plan their tactics and negotiators establish the required degree of trust.

As time draws on, a sympathetic relationship develops between captors and captives and, other things being equal, it becomes harder for the former to kill those they have now come to "know." At least, this is the theory, and in many cases it has proven to be so. The Balcombe Street siege in December 1975, in which IRA terrorists held an elderly couple hostage for six days in a London flat, was ended without bloodshed. The same held true in the Spaghetti House siege, which occurred in London some two months earlier. In this incident, eight hostages were taken by three gunmen who had been interrupted while in the process of robbing an Italian restaurant. The Arab terrorists who hijacked EgyptAir Boeing 737 in November 1985 in Malta intended, however, to kill hostages from the onset and, long after the initial "settling down" period had elapsed, continued to shoot selected passengers. The determining factor as to who should die was, in this instance, possession of a Western passport. Tony Lyons, a Cambridgeshire businessman who was on the aircraft but managed to "stumble" out of a doorway when it was assaulted by Egyptian commandos in an ill-fated rescue effort, said shortly after the event that he was "next in line to be executed by the terrorists." Hami Galal, the aircraft's captain, said of the terrorists that "each time they shot another passenger they joked and danced about it."[5]

Prolonged negotiation in such cases becomes futile when weighed against a mounting toll of dead and injured hostages, and talks are only useful to continue while assault/rescue forces are coordinated and a frontal attack planned.

The Stockholm Syndrome

A fundamental consideration in hostage/siege situations is what is known as the "Stockholm Syndrome," so called after a phenomenon that took place in 1973 during the siege of a Swedish bank where hostages were being held. The leader of the would-be robbers, Jan Erik Olsson, took several hostages during the abortive raid, some of whom were young women. A physical relationship developed in the course of the siege between two of the women and Olsson and another member of the bank-raid team. After the siege, it was found that many of the hostages felt sympathetic toward the perpetrators and were unwilling to condemn them. One of the women explained that she had only allowed a physical relationship to occur in the hope of ending the siege quickly, but many months after the incident she admitted to still feeling affection for him.

The captor/captive bond seems to develop after about two to three days. Although a physical relationship is unusual, general feelings of sympathy, growing, with time, into support, are common. This effect was noticeable among hostages from the Iranian embassy siege in London in 1980, and among some of those from hijacked Flight 847 in 1985. This took place in spite of the fact that on both occasions hostages had been killed. President Duarte of El Salvador was reported as saying that his daughter, upon her release from guerrilla kidnappers, was "suffering" from the syndrome,[6] although, in this case, we might be confusing "unconscious" development of sympathies and affections with the results of applied propaganda techniques. There are points for and against the syndrome, and these may be exploited by either party. On the one hand, the feelings of sympathy for their captors may cause the hostages to deliberately jeopardize rescue efforts made on their behalf. On the other hand, knowledge of the syndrome may cause perpetrators to encourage it, believing (probably correctly) that upon their safe release the hostages will spread only positive, favorable publicity for the "cause."

While the syndrome is a valid and proven phenomenon, it cannot–as we have seen–be relied upon to save lives. The motivation behind a hostage situation and the mental state of the perpetrators will vary from incident to incident.

NOTES

1. J. Bowyer Bell, *A Time of Terror* (New York: Basic Books, 1978), p. 8.
2. Ibid., p. 129.
3. Ibid., pp. 42–43.
4. Ibid., p. 42.
5. *London Times* and others, 25 November 1985.
6. Ibid.

11

Terrorist Technology and Weaponry

Developments in technology have long been of interest to terrorist groups, which have never been slow to consider their suitability for a variety of applications.

A HISTORICAL GLIMPSE

Early nineteenth-century Irish-American terrorists invested some sixty thousand dollars in commissioning the construction of three submarines. Only one was ever completed—in New York by Messrs. Delamater and Company—but it was never employed in a terrorist action. In the 1860s, plans were made for the use of a steamer and a railway train in terrorist operations, but, again, the schemes never materialized.[1] In May 1882, specially imported slaughterhouse knives were used by the Phoenix Park (Dublin) murderer to kill Lord Frederick Cavendish and his private secretary.[2] In 1906 in Russia, Azev, leader of the Social Revolutionaries Fighting Organization, gave Buchalo, an anarchist engineer, twenty thousand rubles to construct an aircraft which he wished to use in a terrorist action. The aircraft was never completed.[3]

Alfred Noble's invention of dynamite in the mid-nineteenth century was hailed as the ultimate in terror technology by anarchists and revolutionaries alike, who imagined its power to be far greater than was the case. In a publication by Johann Most, a noted German radical of the time, it was "revealed" that a dynamite bomb of only ten pounds would destroy any warship.[4] This was soon proven to be a wildly inaccurate prediction. The advent of nitroglycerine/nitrocellulose explosives did, however, facilitate the use of much smaller and more powerful devices than had been possible using black powder. Some of the black-powder devices had been enormous. The Fenian (Irish revolutionary) attack on Clerkenwell prison in December 1867, for example, involved the use of five hundred pounds of black powder. Twelve people were killed in the attack and one hundred and twenty injured.[5]

The use of explosives by terrorists in those early days was to set the pattern for future years. An early "nail bomb" (a barrel full of black powder and metal pieces with a time fuse) was used in an attempt to kill Napoleon while he was still first consul. The attack, by St. Regent, an ex-Navy officer, failed only because the device detonated too late. Russian terrorists of the late nineteenth century contemplated sending "letter bombs" to the tsar. These were to be small parcels of explosive disguised as various medicines. The attacks were, apparently, never initiated.[6]

The first "parcel bomb" was sent in June 1895 by one Paul Koschemann, a twenty-year-old anarchist mechanic. The device, consisting of gunpowder, bottles of ligroin, and a revolver-detonator connected to an alarm clock, was intercepted at a Berlin post office en route to a senior police officer. Romanian terrorists successfully used letter bombs prior to World War I, and terrorists in India in 1908 experimented, without great success, in constructing book bombs. (Such techniques are not as new as we might have thought!)

The advent of plasticized explosive during World War II removed most of the handling problems, which hitherto had taken a steady toll of inexperienced bomb designers and users. More stable, more easily transported, and easily disguised or hidden in innocent-looking objects, plastic explosives soon became the standard tool in covert operations. Reinhard Heydrich, the Nazi Reichsprotektor nicknamed "The Bloody Butcher" because of the cruel and savage techniques he employed against those under his "protection," was killed (on May 26, 1942) by Czech assassins using one of the first plastic-explosive-based bombs.[7] Sheet or slab plastic explosive was also used in the briefcase bomb planted by Colonel Stauffenberg at Hitler's Rastenberg retreat on July 15, 1944. The explosive had actually been taken from captured British commandos some time before and was detonated by an acid delay fuse. Several people were killed in the explosion and many injured, but Hitler himself survived.[8]

TIME-DELAY AND DETONATION DEVICES

Military developments in time-delay and detonation techniques have filtered through to the terrorist user over the years. Before World War I, the German public was warned not to handle anarchist devices with burning fuses for fear that the constructor had incorporated an additional detonation system in the design—an early "booby trap." The burning fuse may still be found in terrorist applications in the form of a safety or blasting fuse, which burns at a rate of around thirty to fifty seconds per foot. Aside from simply lighting such fuses manually, the terrorist may employ firing devices operating on pressure, pressure release, pull friction, pressure friction, chemical, acid-delay/mechanical striker, and a variety of other principles. In this context they will all connect to some form of flash initiator which, when activated, lights the safety fuse or sets off the detonator immediately. The electric detonator lends itself well to countless terrorist applications and may be found in devices ranging from vehicular mines to letter bombs. Miniature and flat-pack batteries and homemade detonators may be employed in this latter type of device to create an extremely inconspicuous finished product.

Incendiary letter bombs have proven popular with many terrorist groups, especially the Middle Eastern and Irish movements, which were responsible for the majority of all such devices sent during the mail-bomb wave of the 1970s.

The IRA has recently generated new fears by demonstrating its ability to plant bombs that are timed to detonate many weeks after their placement. This means that known or suspected political conference sites, for example, can be worked on well in advance of the pre-conference security measures. The technology developed for the home video recorder has provided one of the means for achieving this; the timer units from such devices are designed to switch things on and off at specific times and dates several weeks, months, or even a year after they are set. These "things" can just as easily be the electrical circuit of a bomb as a video recorder. Stand-alone timers can be purchased from many electronic stores for a fraction of what they would have cost four or five years ago. Being microprocessor controlled, these timers are incredibly accurate and reliable. At the time of writing, a stand-alone timer with a self-contained power supply is available which can be set to turn on an "appliance" up to five years ahead.

RADIO-CONTROLLED DEVICES

Radio control is another way in which the terrorist can detonate devices at his leisure. The technique is not new, but again, developments in the field of microelectronics mean that the required equipment is now cheaper and more readily available. An odd variation on radio-control detonation is to be found in some of the Middle Eastern suicide attacks in which the perpetrator/victim drives a vehicle close to the target, where it is detonated by a third party watching from a safe distance. In such applications, radio control negates the risk that the driver might detonate too soon, too late, or in the event of a change of heart, not at all.

An IRA trailer bomb discovered by council workmen in the center of Liverpool, England, in December 1985, was found to be linked to a radio-control detonation system, and jamming signals were quickly set up to prevent the device from detonating while it was being made safe.[9] (A perverse sense of humor is sometimes demonstrated by IRA bombers. In 1977, for example, they initiated an operation which comprised the hijacking of a fleet of bread-delivery vans. Several of these vans were then rigged with explosive devices while others were parked conspicuously on street corners—locked, to prevent easy access and encourage suspicion. Each "bluff" had to be cleared by the security forces as painstakingly as if it were known to contain a bomb. The vehicles that had been rigged, upon detonation, showered a bemused Belfast populace with loaves of bread.)

Radio-control systems are not difficult to construct for anyone with basic knowledge of the field, and there are many books available on the subject. The use of such systems does present some dangers for the truly amateur, however, as stray radio signals from other nearby transmitters may trigger the system accidentally. The more crude the system, the greater this risk is, as even signals on a completely different frequency from that of the detonator contain "harmonics"—multiples of the original transmission frequency—and at close range these may "fool" the detonator into reacting. More sophisticated systems require a two-part, coded signal to be received. These are extremely unlikely to appear by chance and devices so equipped are far safer.

INFANTRY-STYLE WEAPONS

Infantry-style weapons as used by terrorists vary widely in both nature and application. It is the exception rather than the rule that a particular group be armed uniformly. In the terrorist fold, supply-line constraints, financial considerations, and a desire for status projection are often far greater factors in weapons choice than operational applicability.

In open fighting, where the terrorists are, in all but name, irregular soldiers fighting a guerrilla war, the practical limitations on weaponry are availability and access. Difficulties in this latter area are often overcome by the simple military expedient of taking weapons from dead or captured opponents. A situation can occur in which a poorly funded group with little support is able to seize modern, high-quality weapons and turn them against a well-backed, powerful opponent. Other groups rely, in part at least, on donations from sympathetic, but officially non-involved regimes. These regimes may themselves have captured the weapons and deemed it prudent to redistribute these rather than supply more modern, expensive, and traceable weaponry. In Africa especially, this is the case. So prolonged have the actions been in that part of the world, however, and so diverse the supply lines, that one may find weapons dating back to World War II being used alongside those of the most recent manufacture. Reliability and ease of use and maintenance are factors of importance to the user who expects to meet armed resistance while on operations, as are the availability and interchangeability of spare parts. The terrorist engaged in hit-and-runs against unarmed civilians in a modern urban environment, however, will have different priorities, foremost among these being concealability.[10]

For the group operating in a stable urban environment, there are serious problems as regards weapons acquisition and deployment. Immigration/customs controls and policing methods, although far from perfect, obviously serve to limit the nature of weapons that can be used in terrorist operations. Social conventions also play a part: In London, for example, a small shopping bag left unattended outside a department store will attract considerable suspicion; in Beirut, however, the bag would have to make a very large bang indeed before generating similar concern.

On occasion, though, terrorists have succeeded in deploying weapons in urban areas of the West, of a type which one would not normally expect to see outside of an overt war situation. In 1973 Arab terrorists used SAM-7 (heat-seeking, surface-to-air missiles) in an attack against El Al aircraft at Rome airport. Two years later at Orly Airport, Paris, Arab terrorists deployed RPG-2s (Rocket Propelled Grenade) and RPG-7s against the same airline. Both assaults using the Soviet-made weaponry were tactical, if not publicity, failures; and in the Rome incident, a Yugoslavian airliner was actually hit in error. In July 1986, ETA operatives fired six anti-tank grenades at the Spanish Defense Ministry building in Madrid.

"HOMEMADE" WEAPONS

Even where adequate security measures do serve to prevent the terrorists from importing/exporting or purchasing in-country certain types of weapons, they will often resort to do-it-yourself methods. This is well illustrated in Northern Ireland by the IRA. Its on-site construction methods effectively compensate for weapons-denial measures enacted by British security forces and allied intelligence agencies. Homemade grenades—based on shotgun cartridges—and homemade grenade launchers are frequently used in attacks on the British army units patrolling the area, but perhaps the most impressive home-brew weapon in the IRA arsenal is its "Mk 10 Mortar."

Fabricated from cut-off gas cylinders and assorted pieces of angle iron, the mortar tubes are often fired from the back of a hijacked flatbed truck. This provides for maneuverability. It also adds a frighteningly random element to any such attacks, as the downblast of the firing rocket causes the truck to rock from side to side, making for an unpredictable impact pattern. Since its initial deployment some years ago, the Mk 10 has been used in attacks against RUC (Royal Ulster Constabulary) stations and other targets more than eighteen times. Up until February 28, 1985, these attacks resulted in no more than two deaths. The attack on February 28, however, again against an RUC station, killed nine RUC officers, including two Catholics. Since the signing of the Anglo-Irish accord in December 1985, attacks employing this type of weapon and ones of similar ilk have intensified. The targets remain primarily RUC stations.

OFF-THE-SHELF SYSTEMS

Advances in electronics mean that a variety of inexpensive, seemingly innocent "triggers" is now available for possible use in terrorist devices. Some of these systems, which just a few years ago would have been prohibitively expensive and overly large, are now commonly found as the "front end" of intruder detection or area status alarms (alarms which indicate a change in area-status, i.e., whether an area is too hot, too cold, too wet, etc.). The availability of these different kinds of triggers means that the terrorist can now confect a wide variety of high-tech mines, booby traps, and bombs. All he has to do is add the explosives and the detonator to the kind of trigger that suits his purpose, and even these materials can be made from readily available materials. An infrared intruder alarm, for example, when activated by the warmth of a human body, will, via a relay or power transistor, operate a bell or siren. If the circuit output to the bell is instead taken to an on-board explosives-and-detonator package, the presence of a warm body has very different results. All of the modern alarm equipment is based on microcomponents, and there exists plenty of room within the casing for the required additions.

Such systems include the following:

Ultrasonic Detector. This operates on the basis of the

Doppler effect. The Doppler effect in this case could come from the transmission of a 40KHz carrier signal. The reception of that reflected signal plus any additional frequency-shifted signals coming from the presence of a target would trigger the explosion.

Radar Doppler Detector. Common models operate on around 10.7 GHz and function by measuring the difference between transmitted and reflected radio frequencies. They are not susceptible to interference from sound or light sources and may be hidden behind thin plastic or card, through which the needed signals will pass. The reaction range is usually adjustable from two meters to about twenty meters.

Fluid Detector. Various fluid detector integrated circuits are now available which are an improvement over the older stand-alone hygrometric devices. Selling for as little as fifteen dollars, these systems might be placed part way down a water cistern, so as to trigger an explosion when the water level drops; or in drains in such a manner as to trigger when it next rains. There are many possibilities.

Electronic Thermostat. These could be employed in locations where changes of temperature are predictable. They could be placed on a roof, for example, so as to trigger when the sun rises or sets; or atop a vehicle exhaust pipe, so as to trigger when the engine has been running for some time. Small and easily portable, these devices may be very accurately set.

Photovoltaic Cells. These small units convert light into electric current. They might be placed during the hours of darkness to go off at daybreak. Alternatively, they could be placed so as to activate when struck by a source of artificial light, such as the beam from a police officer's torch as he searches for signs of a reported break-in. They might even be placed in a garage area, so as to trigger when hit by the headlights of a vehicle.

Sound-Activated Devices. These can be found designed to operate within the normal audio spectrum or just outside it (ultrasonic/subsonic). A possible application is a deadly version of the surveillance "infinity bug," in which a device planted inside a telephone is activated by remote control by calling the host number and either before or after it is answered, sending a tone down the line. The tone may be electronically generated, or produced by a single-note "harmonica." In the surveillance application, the tone opens up the telephone microphone insert. In the terrorist version, it instead operates a miniature switch and detonates a chunk of explosive hidden in the phone body or the handset itself. In this latter instance, the effects are reported to be very dramatic indeed. Variations of the technique were apparently used by Israeli operatives against Fedayeen members in Europe.[11]

Theatrical Pyrotechnical Devices. These, in the form of "stage bangs" or "bombs" can easily be pressed into service as makeshift detonators. Such items can be purchased with ease by anyone. Many such devices are electrically fired, and the firing-circuit components available for stage use duplicate almost totally the function of commercial blasting systems. Thus the terrorist has legal and easy access to booby-trap-type initiation systems detonators.

If none of the above devices are available, detonators can even be made from automobile light bulbs, carefully drilled or filed into without damaging the filament. "Bullseye" or some similar smokeless powder is then poured into the bulb. When the circuit is energized, the smokeless powder ignites—simplicity itself. The explosive material can also be very simple. It can be as simple as sugar and ammonium nitrate fertilizer. It could also be potassium permanganate, aluminum or even potassium chlorate, and sulphur, kerosene, or nitrobenzine. There are a variety of other possible combinations.

An inability to access the latest in military technology may frustrate the terrorist, then; but as for preventing him from killing and maiming selected targets—never. The wooden pistol or homemade grenade launcher might not look as effective as its factory-made counterparts, but such weapons continue to claim lives on a regular basis.

NON-WEAPON WEAPONS

Also worthy of consideration in the context of terrorist and counterterrorist technology are the recently developed "non-weapons." These, while not conforming to any of the established weaponry parameters, are able to disorient, disable, and kill. Such devices utilize the effects of sound and radio-frequency energy, among other things. They are of concern because, not being weapons in the traditional sense, they are not subject to controls.

Sound Weapons

Sound weapons rely for their effect, as the name suggests, on the creation and direction of sounds of a certain frequency and pressure. The sounds we experience every day are a combination of frequency and pressure. The combined result is commonly referred to as loudness. Even at quite acceptable levels, sound (noise if you prefer) can cause the lining of the brain and stomach to become inflamed, the small blood vessels to constrict, and the head to ache. Noise can also cause the flow of blood to the heart to be restricted and can seriously affect eyesight.

Very loud and/or high frequency sounds are dangerous, but extremely low-frequency sounds–those below the normal hearing range–are deadly. These low-frequency (infrasonic) sounds produce vibrations which cause the internal organs to rub together. This effect was exploited a few years ago in the movies with the introduction of "sense-surround" sound tracks accompanying certain disaster films. Bass hi-fi speakers for sale in many stores even have reference to the effect in their advertising blurbs–"for wall-shaking bass you can really feel."[12] Several years ago, in Marseilles, France, a team of scientists almost killed themselves and fellow listeners while testing an infrasonic sound weapon. Fortunately, the device was turned off before any lasting damage was done.[13]

The technology required to construct such systems is not complex and can be purchased from any specialist audio store. Once the frequencies involved reach certain levels, the danger becomes immediate. The frequency of 7Hz (7 cycles per second), for example, can be fatal as it is the same frequency as some natural brain-wave rhythms. Such units, mounted atop high buildings or at strategic points along a border area, could cause untold damage before anyone realized what was happening—assuming they ever did. Buildings and structures of all kinds can also be damaged by such weapons. Sound can destroy an office block as surely as a conventional explosive; however, the practical obstacles to using sound against nonliving targets have not yet—as far as I can determine—been fully overcome.

Electro Magnetic Field (EMF) Weapons

In January 1976, the United States government ordered the installation of equipment in its Moscow embassy to defend its occupants from a particular kind of Soviet attack. The equipment was installed as part of Project Pandora. Since the 1950s, the Soviets had been irradiating the embassy with microwave signals. Project Pandora was launched by the U.S. government in the 1950s following the discovery of a mysterious signal at the embassy, located during a debugging sweep. The purpose of the project was to ascertain exactly what, if anything, the signal was doing. At the time, embassy personnel were not informed of the signal's presence or of the project, and blood samples taken from them were justified as being part of the "Moscow viral study," which had been established to determine the cause of a stomach complaint from which many of the embassy employees were suffering. The signals continued and were monitored on a day-to-day basis by intelligence personnel. In 1975 the signals changed as two new transmission sites were established by the Soviets. When the latest in a series of unsuccessful overtures to the Soviets by the U.S. government had failed to persuade them to discontinue the irradiation, it was decided that defensive screens would be fitted.[14]

The embassy staff now had to be informed of the affair, and several of the unhappy employees complained to the press. Subsequent publicity revealed a belief that the two signals converged at a point inside the embassy directly over the head of a golf-ball-type typewriter, and that the reflected signals were being decoded by the Soviets, enabling them to monitor the correspondence typed on that machine. While this satisfied some, a second school of thought developed, holding that the signals were actually being used as a weapon. Exposure to microwave energy can cause various biological effects, including central-nervous-system disturbance, a drop-off in decision-making ability, the generation of chronic stress, etc. At high levels, of course, such energy causes much more serious illness; cancer is thought to be the consequence of exposure to high levels for prolonged periods. While not admitting publicly that anything of a dangerous nature was occurring at the embassy, the government declared it "a stressful post" and gave the workers an extra 20 percent hardship allowance. The government knew, however, that a 1975 survey showed the embassy staff to have a white blood cell count 40 percent higher than normal. Two of the last four ambassadors have subsequently died of cancer and a third has developed a rare blood disease.[15]

It would have been impossible for the U.S. government to admit to a belief of danger at the embassy in any event, as the levels of radiation measured there were far less than those declared by the government to be dangerous in other contexts. Stating publicly that such low levels could do any harm at all would have thrown a shadow of a doubt over the validity of the entire American microwave safety figures. In a survey called "Operation Big Boy," the Project Pandora team found that microwave energy levels on-board U.S. aircraft carriers were a hundred times greater than those in the embassy.[16] The validity of microwave-exposure standards in the United States and many other countries is constantly being challenged in the courts. Although at least twenty-five servicemen who flew on U.S. spy planes in the 1960s and subsequently developed cancers and cataracts won huge out-of-court settlements from microwave equipment manufacturers and operators, such organizations still deny liability.

Dr. Karel Marha, a Czech scientist who defected to the West in the early 1970s, devoted much research to the effects of pulsed electromagnetic fields on animals and humans. In one experiment, even a few seconds of exposure to such a field caused agitation in the subject animal, which was clearly trying to escape the field. After two minutes of exposure, the animal went into a convulsive fit; and after three minutes it died. In tests repeated since, it has been discovered that if the field is turned off just before this final stage, the animal recovers and shows no obvious signs of its experience. A 1976 American intelligence report entitled "Biological Effects of Electromagnetic Radiation (Radiowaves and Microwaves), Eurasian Communist Countries (U) DST-1810S-074-76," mentions that the Soviets at that time saw great potential in the use of microwaves for disorienting American military and diplomatic personnel. It further stated that the Soviets had found a microwave frequency which caused heart seizure in animals, and that a frequency which affected humans in a similar fashion could be determined. The information cutoff date for this report was October 1975, and we can assume that further progress has since been made in this field.

In a September 1978 report, American scientist Dr.

Robert Beck notes specific frequencies causing confusion, fear, anxiety, and, of course, death. He has himself constructed wristwatch-size devices that can provoke various physiological reactions in persons subjected to their output. In a classic experiment, one such device caused fellow diners in a restaurant to talk more loudly or more quietly. By affecting human brain waves, perhaps tuning them to a different frequency, it is possible to alter mood. From this it is a short step to the manipulation of an individual's character. With the Soviets at the forefront of such developments, one wonders how long it will be before they pass on the benefits of their long research and development campaigns to terrorist active-service units for final field-testing.[17]

NOTES

1. Walter Laqueur, *Terrorism* (Weidenfield and Nicolson, 1977), p. 94.
2. Brian McConnel, *Assassination* (London: Leslie Frewin, 1969), p. 147.
3. Walter Laqueur, p. 95.
4. Ibid., p. 93.
5. Ibid., p. 92.
6. Ibid., p. 94.
7. Brian McConnel, p. 241.
8. Ibid., p. 233.
9. *Beacon Radio,* independent local radio broadcasts in England, December 1985.
10. Terror groups will, of course, use whatever weaponry becomes available; but certain types of ordnance have become associated with particular movements, primarily due to media publicity. Thus the Red Brigade elements in Europe with a penchant for the Walther automatic pistol have earned themselves the nickname the "P-38ers"; and reference to the IRA immediately

conjures up images of a brandished Armalite AR-15. The IRA favor their American-made weapon for reasons other than its lightness and accuracy. It can, in fact, be readily "broken" into two "halves" upon removal of a locking pin. It can subsequently be reassembled without losing its zeroing accuracy. That is because both front and rear sights remain attached to the front half of the weapon when it is thus taken apart. The operative who has a sniping attack to mount, then, can zero the weapon to suit himself at some point remote from the intended area of operations, break the weapon, convey it to the area of operations, and reassemble it quickly, confident that the sights remain set. There are other rifles with this capability, and they too lend themselves well to terrorist use. Broken into two parts, the weapons may be concealed in hiding places that would be too small for the fully assembled rifle. Hiding weapons parts beneath a baby in a pram or pushchair is a popular IRA tactic.

The Kalashnikov, with its distinctive curved magazine, has come to symbolize revolution and defiance in several parts of the world—most notably those subject to Soviet influence. One learns a good deal about demonstrators' frame of mind and true intent when one sees home-carved, wooden "weapons" modeled on the AK-47 and its variants being brandished at funerals or so-called peaceful demonstrations. A recent example of this is visible in footage of South African unrest, shown before the 1985 news-control measures.

11. J. Bowyer Bell, *A Time of Terror* (New York: Basic Books, 1978), pp. 79–80, 82, 87–88, 171–73.

12. See, for example, various Radio Shack catalog advertisements.

13. *Illustrated London News:* "Ordeal by Noise," Freedom of Information Act. See, for example, notes pertaining to the *Pandora* meeting of 12 May, 1959, between the Science Advisory Committee and the Walter Reed Army Institute of Research. Also IDA (Institute of Defence Analysis) review panel report of

the *Pandora/Bizarre* briefing, 20 December 1968.

14. From declassified *Pandora* documents.

15. *Pandora* documents.

16. *Pandora* documents.

17. Although the Soviets appear to be genuinely involved with such techniques on a large scale, the private sector in the United States has already produced variants on the aforementioned "psychotronic" weapons that may be found advertised in certain specialist magazines; *Soldier of Fortune,* for example.

12

Executive Protection and Vehicular Kidnapping

As many instances of terrorism can be defined as attacks by one element of the private sector against another, it seems hardly surprising that for some time a major part of the private sector has organized itself with a view to preventing or negating the effects of such attacks. Italy probably still has the largest percentage of bodyguards and related operatives per head of population compared to other countries. This seems well justified when one considers that, on the average, two kidnappings occur weekly in that particular part of the world. Bodyguards—executive-protection operatives, personnel-security consultants, call them what you will—are available in a variety of shapes and sizes to suit any occasion. While they are still to be found, the trend these days is away from the six-foot-six-inch, two-hundred-pound strong-arm men, whose only use would be in a one-on-one unarmed struggle. More usually, the bodyguard of today is a business-suited operative who, while not looking special, is a highly skilled and motivated individual.

Among the best of such operatives, the consensus of opinion is that the main part of the job in personal protection situations is prevention rather than "cure." Assessing potential risks, weighing these against the measures that must be taken to negate them, and generally thinking ahead are the key functions. The services of such people can undoubtedly prove to be a worthwhile investment. A high-risk individual is unlikely to be able to concentrate on his job and still properly oversee his own protection. Thus the calm and calculating security operative, with his mind free to concentrate entirely on the task of protecting his client—anticipating potentially dangerous situations and steering his charge away from them—is a much sought-after commodity in today's risk-filled world. Maintaining a low profile, the bodyguard acts as a human alarm system, a system triggered by events or possible events that the client/target would normally overlook. Complacency with regard to personal security has been the downfall of many.

On January 8, 1971, then British ambassador to Uruguay, Geoffrey Jackson, set out for his office as he had done many times before. Neither he nor his driver, Hugo, thought anything suspicious was going on when they were delayed en route by delivery vehicles loading and unloading merchandise. After all, they had been delayed by such vehicles on several previous occasions. This time, however, a large red van drove right into them. As Hugo climbed out of the vehicle to take down particulars, a young man appeared and struck him across the head. A second terrorist began firing an automatic weapon, and the kidnapping was on. In classic style, the terrorists had predicted the route of the target vehicle, intercepted it, and brought it to a halt without attracting suspicion. Then they seized their victim. One of the terrorist machine gunners, a young woman, had concealed the weapon in a fruit basket. This last detail was a refinement of which, according to Geoffrey Jackson, the terrorists were extremely proud.[1]

It is apparent that in scenarios similar to that described above, the bodyguard's size and personal arsenal become irrelevant. Very little, save for some hasty defensive driving, can be done to rectify such a situation. A bodyguard skilled in such techniques should be the rule rather than the exception. Vehicular attacks are common. As a matter of fact, the majority of assaults against nonmilitary personnel takes place in or nearby automobiles. Broadly speaking, such attacks will follow two patterns, the most basic being an all-out assault on the vehicle with the intention of killing its occupants. The second, as we have seen, requires the slowing and stopping of the vehicle in such a manner as not to provoke the suspicion of the occupants. In this way, the target person may be taken alive, or his death can be assured without doubt.

The following measures are fundamental to the safety of persons liable to attack in a mobile situation. They are among those taught at defensive driving schools (although at some such centers, the evasion techniques are considered to be secondary to the driving techniques themselves).

First and foremost is intelligent route planning. If the potential target is traveling alone or with a single bodyguard–no support vehicles–such planning becomes absolutely critical. Regular journeys to the same place via the same route enable a terrorist group to predict accurately where and when a target will be at a given time. This, of course, facilitates easy ambush. The routes should be varied as much as possible according to no set pattern. The number of persons aware of the chosen route should be kept to a minimum. Employers, for example, will be advised of the route and estimated time of arrival, in order that an overdue arrival automatically sets the warning bells ringing. A simple code may be devised to enable this information to be communicated to those at the destination without revealing it to persons who may be employing surveillance techniques.

En route, obvious ambush locations should be avoided as much as possible. These include service stations, roadside halts, roadworks requiring the stopping of the vehicle, and large vehicles parked as if they have broken down. Drivers standing near parked vehicles and waving for assistance should be ignored, as should apparent hitchhikers or persons asking for directions. Road sections that necessitate slowing of the vehicle to walking pace—hairpin bends, etc.—should also be treated with caution, especially if they coincide with high roadside fences or walls. If such locations cannot be avoided, a road position opposite to the normal one can be adopted. Driving on the "wrong" side of the road—where prevailing traffic conditions permit—will often defeat an attack relying for success on a particular vehicle position.

Also qualifying as potential threats are vehicles seen en route which appear to be waiting at junctions and intersections for no apparent reason. A vehicle seen edging out of a side road in front of the potential target vehicle that has sufficient room and time to complete the maneuver before the target nears it, but instead waits and pulls out behind, could be part of an attack team moving into position. Large or heavy vehicles which seem to time their maneuver to coincide with the arrival on scene of the potential target justify an immediate about-turn. Suspicions will soon be confirmed or proven incorrect according to whether or not that same vehicle appears in the rear-view mirror.

Tails, established sometimes to follow the target until a suitable ambush point is reached, are readily identified by keeping a constant watch on traffic behind and in front of one's vehicle. Front tailing is somewhat more difficult than the more usual rear type, but a skillful driver or team (driver and navigator) with even a basic idea of the intended route of the target can employ the technique with remarkable success. This technique becomes easier when the target is traveling on long straight highways where the possible maneuvers open to him are limited. A police driver with whom I discussed this subject recently explained that a possible target who suspects a tail will usually continue to look for another suspicious vehicle following him from behind once a vehicle passes him in normal fashion that he suspects is in reality a tail. Tailing, apparently, in the majority of minds, means someone behind and not in front.

Making a sudden turn, of course, will lose and/or reveal the presence of any tail immediately, but several such maneuvers during the course of the journey will be required to lose tails employing more than one vehicle. Where this technique is used, a group will often employ radio communication to stay in touch and relay instructions to fellow members. The frequent appearance, then, of two or more vehicles displaying antennas of a similar or identical design may imply the presence of a radio-linked tail.

There are various devices on the market which enable a potential target to ensure—to some degree—his speedy location in the event of kidnap. The common type is simply a radio transmitter which sends out signals to a receiver. The electronic "shape" of the signal indicates the direction of the transmitter. If an executive, for example, fails to arrive on schedule, a vehicle equipped with a suitable receiver—or several vehicles for greater speed—can be sent out along the proposed route. The transmitter end of such systems can be extremely small, and easily disguised as an innocent item such as a watch, lighter, or pen. The price to be paid for this miniaturization, however, is that signals will not travel great distances. Even so, assuming a search team gets close to the area in which the hostage is being held, the use of such devices would represent a great improvement over a purely physical search. This becomes obvious when one considers, for example, that Geoffrey Jackson's kidnappers kept him hidden below ground in a well-concealed "prison."[2]

For individuals traveling a regular, established route, perhaps from home to office, a receiver may be permanently located at the office. At an arranged time it could be switched on to track the approach of the executive. It is not necessary to be limited to "control" signals—those usually received when all is well and the journey uninterrupted. It is possible to use such devices in a way that permits one to determine that no untoward deviation or delay is occurring. There are in fact many ways in which such devices may be used. Small, body-worn units may be set to trigger a silent alarm in the event of a kidnap or other threatening situation. Here again, the drastic fall in the cost of technology of late has meant it is possible to establish this type of protection at levels previously reserved for only very high-ranking company executives or government employees. Currently a fair percentage of all intruder alarm calls are answered initially by a private response company, which then contacts the police if necessary. It is probable that the future will see "kidnap alarms" responded to in a similar manner. The company or wealthy individual will enlist the services of a full-time protection agency, which will be a cross between the conventional bodyguard company and an electronic-surveillance agency.

It is illegal in several countries to pay a ransom to kidnappers. Even where such payments are not actually illegal, they are frowned upon by police departments for obvious reasons. The instances of kidnap in which the proviso for the release of the hostage is *not* payment of a large ransom are few and far between. As many of the most successful kidnaps in recent years have only ended without loss of life because such demands have been met and the police and other law-enforcement agencies excluded from the affair completely, the majority of large companies conclude that this is the safest way to handle such events. The same can be said of the relatives of potential targets. It seems even more likely, therefore, that the private sector will retain a strong involvement with such situations in the foreseeable future.

NOTES

1. Geoffrey Jackson, *People's Prison* (London: Faber and Faber, 1973), p. 28.
2. Ibid., p. 81.

13

The Antiterrorist Arsenal

One area in which the private sector has not been slow to establish a foothold is the design and supply of weaponry and support equipment for protection against terrorists. This chapter considers the technology and techniques behind some of the more interesting advances that have been made in this field over the past few years.

SURVEILLANCE

A spin-off of medical research that has played an important part in many terrorist siege incidents of late is the miniature, fiber-optic camera. Developed originally to facilitate the viewing of a patient's lung or stomach wall, these tiny units are often as small as 11 millimeters in diameter with an aperture requirement of only 1.5mm–about the same size as the tip of a ballpoint pen. Equipment such as this was used by the British police's C7 (technical support) division during the Spaghetti House siege in London in October 1975. The siege came about when gunmen attempting to rob an Italian restaurant in Knightsbridge were trapped by the police. The police were called by one of the restaurant-chain managers, who had been on the premises counting some $20,000 in receipts when the raiders burst in and had managed to get away. Realizing their predicament, the gunmen seized the remaining eight managers hostage and barricaded themselves in a basement storeroom. As initial negotiations were taking place, C7 operatives first installed audio-surveillance devices and then the first of two video units. One of these cameras was snaked around some water pipes that entered the storeroom; the other was inserted through the side of a metal ventilating duct. In this latter case, a hole was burned through the vent with acid dripping slowly from an eye dropper into a dam of self-adhesive material. This took several hours of patient work, but when the hole was finally complete and the camera head inserted, the police were able to monitor every movement and comment within the storeroom. It was thus possible to observe the mental state of both hostages and captors and determine a suitable reaction policy. All hostages were eventually released unharmed.

In the following month, the Metropolitan police were able to share their experience—and the equipment—with the Irish Garda (police), when Dutch industrialist Dr. Tiede Herrema was kidnapped and held hostage by the IRA. Once again, the miniature television equipment was put to good use, enabling the security forces to watch and listen to events clearly as they occurred inside the siege building. The video recording of this incident is still used as an Irish police training film. In the Dutch train sieges in December 1975 and May 1977, similar equipment was employed, and, in the 1977 incident, Special Air Service elements were sent to help install the electronic devices and advise generally on the situation.

Possibilities for the future include the permanent installation of such equipment in high-risk areas (embassies, for example). The camera and its related electronics would, of course, be well concealed and only those with a real need to know informed of its presence or exact location. Should a siege or other terrorist situation develop, valuable time could be saved, since the reaction force would need only to connect up the reception/monitoring end of the link.

BUGS

Concealed microphones–linked to the listener or a recording device via wires or a radio transmitter–have been employed in a counterterrorist function for some time. Their application as a military tool at least goes as far back as World War I, when wire-linked microphones were used to monitor enemy troop movement on the battlefield. During World War II, hidden microphones in prison cells and work areas were used to monitor the conversations of interned German nuclear scientists. Since that time, the development of related technology has been continuous, and the results quite staggering. The range of miniature bugs available to anyone who might care to purchase them is enormous. While some at the lower end of the scale are cheap devices with limited professional application potential, the state-of-the-art systems can effectively mean the difference between success and failure in a variety of counter-terrorist scenarios.

The laser bug is perhaps one of the most exotic of the newer types to see active service, including, reputedly, at the Balcombe Street siege in London in December 1975. This was an incident in which an elderly couple was held hostage by IRA terrorists for not quite six days. The device–which can be constructed to resemble a variety of innocent-looking objects, a camera being a popular design–is pointed at a window in the target building that reflects the transmitted beam of light. Imposed on this reflected beam is the pattern of any conversation or sound being made in the room behind the window. By decoding these signals electronically, they can be turned back into recognizable speech. East German security forces reportedly use this type of equipment, and an infrared unit is available, meaning that the beam of light is not visible to the naked eye. In the late 1970s, these devices were available in England for about two thousand dollars.

Conventional bugs appear on the market regularly in the form of tie clips, pens, electric-socket adaptors, belt buckles, desk sets, matchboxes, lighters, picture frames (in which the frame itself contains the antenna), and a variety of other objects. Many suppliers will custom-build a bug into the item of a customer's choice, and this means that such units may be found literally anywhere. Some of the bugs operate constantly, while others are triggered only when a sound is made nearby or on receipt of a radio signal or audio tone. These remotely activated bugs are almost impossible to find without special equipment. The cheaper types frequently operate in the 90 to 110 megahertz range, meaning they can be tuned to by anyone with a domestic radio receiver. More professional versions can attain 600 megahertz and utilize sub-carrier techniques, which means that, even if someone should tune to the signal by accident or during a sweep using standard equipment, he would not actually hear any audio and could thus well assume that the signal was "innocent." Bugs employed by the police and military at the Iranian embassy siege in London in May 1980 provided vital intelligence. It is safe to conclude that any siege location could be similarly bugged without the knowledge of the perpetrators.

This seems especially true when one considers a recent development known familiarly as "the superbug," a version of which is produced by the British Home Office Directorate of Telecommunications. In an account of a drugs-squad operation headed by Detective Chief Inspector Lee (which successfully closed down a major international narcotics production and smuggling ring), this listening device is described as so powerful it can monitor every conversation within the target building, with all the doors and windows shut, from a considerable distance away. So powerful is this device, that written permission from a Home Office minister has to be obtained before it can be used in an operation. In the operation in question–Operation

Julie—the application for its use was denied.[1]

That such devices are considered worthy of close control by the British government should not be taken to imply that they are not available in an equally powerful form from other sources. The widespread availability of various bugging devices poses the following question: What is to stop the terrorists from turning this technology back on those who would use it against them? The answer, of course, is absolutely nothing. It may only be a matter of time before the hijackers of a commercial airliner greatly compromise actions against them by employing such devices. A "superbug" in the flight deck of the hijacked aircraft, for example, would surely enable the terrorists to monitor control-tower conversations as well as those occurring among reaction-team personnel in the immediate area. Easier still would be the placement by a terrorist sympathizer of a more conventional device in or near the control tower. With decisions on the part of security forces and advisors known by the terrorists as soon as they were made, the situation would be almost impossible to resolve satisfactorily. At the least, such techniques would enable the terrorists to determine precisely what they can or cannot expect to get away with. Thus any bargaining would become decidedly one-sided.

TELEPHONE TAPS

Telephone tapping is the cornerstone of many current-day counterterrorist operations. The practice is far from new. In 1914, the many miles of field-telephone wire laid by both German and British forces were regularly cut into, and the passing information monitored. By 1915, the Germans had developed an amplifier which could detect the ground component of the telephone system, thereby obviating the need to splice into the wires at all. This in turn provoked the design and construction of one of the first jamming devices, a unit which produced electrical "noise" which could be transmitted into the ground near to a receiver. On the first day of World War I (August 5, 1914), the British ship *Telconia* was sent out into the North Sea to disable German trans-Atlantic telephone cables. This done, the Germans were obliged to route their distant communications via radio or other cables, all of which could be accessed at will by the British and the Americans.

In 1953 the CIA (Central Intelligence Agency) and British intelligence agencies put into effect an equally subtle operation, which involved the digging of a tunnel from Rudow in West Berlin some half a mile across the border into Alt Glienicke in East Berlin. This enabled CIA communications personnel to tap into the main telephone cables running from East Berlin to Leipzig. Many messages from the East German Army headquarters were thus intercepted. The taps functioned well apparently until 1976, when the arrival of legitimate telephone engineers prompted a hasty CIA retreat.

Telephone taps might still be installed in target premises, but in the majority of counterterrorist operations they will be switched on at the exchange or some other official listening station. An exception will arise in the case of operations not considered sufficiently important to warrant the official sanctioning of such techniques. Most modern exchanges have "TKO" boards—or similar design features, which facilitate immediate tapping in to a subscriber's line to check for faults or to enable itemized phone billing.

The equipment capable of producing itemized phone bills for individual subscribers—the TXE2 and TXE4, for example—automatically record every number called. As such, they are effective nontap taps. The terrorist suspect, or convicted terrorist recently released from prison, is quite likely to be the subject of telephone surveillance conducted by these means, as in most instances no warrant would be required. Some exchanges employ what is known as a transit system (in England, this is called MF2) which allows certain users to dial into another occupied line. In effect this means that with the "correct" sequence of digits, an investigating officer could dial a busy number and, instead of receiving the busy tone, would be able to listen to the conversation in progress. At the British Army headquarters in Lisburn, Northern Ireland, there exists a listening office through which all telephone calls can be switched into by computer and recorded. Not surprisingly, the office is under constant military guard. It is no secret, also, that certain British military personnel, frustrated at times by official constraints on surveillance operations, purchase their own tapping equipment and conduct such projects on what might be called a free-lance basis.

In the United States, the National Security Agency is reported to monitor all international calls emanating from the U.S. and record for subsequent analysis a large percentage of them.[2] Speech-recognition techniques are under constant evaluation at the NSA, which admitted investing seven million dollars in the field in 1973. Speech-recognition systems are designed to react to certain programmed trigger words, such as bomb, drugs, and assassinate. Reception of such words automatically starts a recorder and alerts the personnel. In 1977, the British Home Office purchased a voice-recognition computer for the police scientific development branch from the American company, Threshold. This same company has also sold equipment to the British GCHQ (Government Communications Headquarters), at Cheltenham.

BOMB DISPOSAL

As an aid to the detection of explosive devices, various "sniffer" units have been designed and developed. These facilitate the rapid location of hidden explosive material, including ammunition. One such device, Explosives Detector L1A1, made by Rye Dynamics Ltd., in cooperation with the RARDE (Royal Armament Research and Development Establishment), Fort Holland, Kent, comprises a backpack, inert-gas cylinder, and hand-held sensor head. Small amounts of air are sucked into the unit via the head and analyzed. If any explosive substance is detected, a small white light flashes and an audio signal is triggered. The sampling cycle takes only sixteen seconds.

A company called the SAS Group produces a device known as Chemitec which will detect homemade explosives.[3] It is currently in use by the British Army and police. Many such detectors are sensitive enough to detect explosives on a suspect's hands even after they have been washed. Their most suitable application is in the detection of explosives hidden in an item which could otherwise only be searched by destroying or seriously damaging it. The large plants common in many airport reception lounges, for example, make for ideal terrorist bomb-concealment locations. Prior to the development of the electronic sniffer, they could only be checked by dogs or by physically emptying out the plant and its container.

If an explosive device is found, it can be examined safely by the ordnance-disposal operative with a robot explosives-ordnance vehicle. The most common of these machines are the Felix Wheelbarrow, made by Morfax Ltd., and the Marauder. Such robots are tracked vehicles–able to negotiate steps and rough terrain–which are guided to the bomb or suspicious object by the operator via a closed-circuit television link. The remote-controlled facilities on board include full speed and steering capability, mechanical grab "hands," and a rifle or shotgun discharger. Thus the unit is remotely maneuvered to its target, where it can relay visual information to its operator, blast open a car door or the lock on a suitcase, cut through the wires on a device, and so on. Interchangeable attachments facilitate the performance of numerous tasks. The Felix Wheelbarrow costs just under twenty thousand dollars. At least forty have been destroyed while dealing with terrorist bombs in Northern Ireland.

DOGS

The use of dogs in counterterrorist operations is quite widespread. There are few security-force groups that do not have at least access to suitably trained canine helpers. Some police departments rely on private breeders to supply the animals; others breed their own. The types of breed most commonly used by police and military include boxers, Rottweilers, Dobermans, Reisenschnausers, Labradors, Bouviers, and of course, the German shepherd (Alsatian). The trend currently is toward special-skill dogs, i.e., one dog for one task rather than "do it all" animals. Consequently some dogs are trained to sniff for drugs, others for firearms, and others for the buried remains of murder victims. The dog's highly developed sense of smell has made it popular also in man-tracking scenarios following kidnappings or prison escapes.

In addition to the sniffing role, dogs are trained for aggressor applications. Scotland Yard, as an example, has a dozen or so antiterrorist dogs, specially trained to be vicious and unafraid of gunfire or explosions. They are comparable, one suspects, to the "war dog" of earlier vintage. It is interesting to note that the Special Air Service is trained in anti-dog techniques, and on occasion has attracted adverse publicity by putting such techniques into practice during various military exercises. "MK ULTRA" documents (which relate to CIA-sponsored mind control and guided animal studies) from the 1960s show that the CIA at that time considered using radio-controlled dogs for "direct executive action-type operations." This is intelligence parlance for assassination. The dogs in this instance were to be controlled via brain implants linked to a radio system.[4] Upon receipt of a certain type of signal, the animals would respond in a certain way. The technique was tested some years ago and works. In a classic demonstration, a charging bull is made to stop in its tracks by sending a radio signal to a receiver implanted in its brain. With the transmitter off, the bull again charges; once the signal is sent, it stops immediately. It is indeed a disturbing phenomenon to witness.

By utilizing similar techniques, or simply force-feeding an animal an explosive and radio-controlled detonator system—easy enough when using miniature components and a large dog—a terrorist target could be subjected to "direct-executive action" with far fewer risks than would be the case if employing human operatives. The scenario that springs most readily to mind is that of a doctored animal running out across the airfield toward the targeted person as he disembarks from an aircraft. Security guards would think little of such an incident. Save for perhaps half-heartedly shooing the creature aside, they would probably take no action. In a perfectly natural fashion, the target stoops to pat the animal, which now sits and pants happily at his feet. Some yards away a small red button is pressed, and dog and target are no more.

Animals could also be used to plant surveillance devices. There are a number of possibilities applicable both to terrorist and counterterrorist scenarios. As a CIA memo from the 1960s on the subject says, "this gets very exotic very fast."

NONLETHAL WEAPONS

As a large percentage of terrorist–security-force confrontations involve risk to bystanders and hostages, the search for weapons that will overpower and disable (but not kill) is ongoing. Such weapons are the more important because provoking overreaction on the part of government and security forces is a definite terrorist aim. The "unnecessary" death of even a self-confessed terrorist often serves to encourage more support for the terrorist cause. Thus security forces in many cases try to put down terrorist-backed riots with force short of the fatal. While there are weapons that are classified here as nonlethal, this refers only to the fact that they are not designed to inflict fatal injury and, if used as suggested by manufacturers, will not do so. In the heat of riot or rescue situations, however, operatives seldom have the time to judge safe ranges or take precise aim. Consequently, people have died after being hit by plastic bullets (baton rounds), and others have choked to death on "nonlethal" gas.[5]

There is continuing cooperation between the United States and Britain on nonlethal as well as lethal weapons and techniques. Operatives from both countries frequently meet to discuss and assess new developments. American companies are aware that Northern Ireland presents an ideal opportunity to test or demonstrate weapons of varying types and are not slow to offer their products for field-testing there.

Stun Bag

One of the more peculiar of nonlethal weapons evaluated in recent years was the "stun bag." This weapon was comprised of a special gun and its projectile, which somewhat resembled a child's bean bag. This padded bag contained 100 to 350 grams of lead shot which, when fired from a 40-millimeter container-cartridge, spread the bag out to a diameter of about 100 centimeters. Within an effective range of sixty meters, the stun bag had an impact energy of around one hundred footpounds—very similar to that of a plastic bullet at a range of fifty yards. Manufactured by M. B. Associates of San Raman, California, the weapon was rejected by American agencies as having too high an impact energy for its intended role—wounding rioters. The stun bag was demonstrated to British army officers at the army headquarters in Northern Ireland, but its use was never recommended.

Plastic Bullets

The plastic bullet (baton round) remains the primary weapon in many riot situations where it has been decided that shooting to kill with lethal ammunition will bring more harm than good. Typically, the plastic bullet is made from PVC (polyvinyl chloride), and is about four inches long, and an inch-and-a-quarter in diameter. It looks like a flatnosed candle and weighs about five ounces. Plastic bullets can be fired from a variety of weapons and are accurate to around fifty meters. The round itself comprises the hard PVC bullet, an aluminum case, a plastic charge capsule, and a central percussion cap. Unlike the earlier rubber bullets, plastic rounds are intended to be fired directly at the target, albeit at the lower part of the body. Thus mob ring leaders can be incapacitated quickly, with minimal risk of permanent injury or death.

In the United States, an interesting variation on the plastic/rubber bullet appeared in the late 1970s in the form of the Sting RAG projectile. This was an impact-energy weapon comprised of a soft rubber ring some two-and-a-half inches in diameter. It had a single-target accuracy of around forty-five yards.

Sound Curdler

First used by American police during the 1968 college campus riots, this device consists of a sound source, a high-power amplifier, and a speaker assembly. It produces a high-pitched shrieking noise at irregular intervals and can be mounted on vehicles or helicopters. These units can be used for verbal communication over large distances–about two miles for the 350-watt version. They are more commonly used to establish a modulated sound blanket which makes it impossible for riot coordinators to communicate their instructions. Thirteen such units, HPSI systems, have been purchased by the British government for deployment in Northern

Ireland. They are made by Applied Electro Mechanics, Alexandria, Virginia, and cost around four thousand dollars each.

Squawk Box

This consists of two high-power ultrasonic transmitters operating on slightly different frequencies. Although the majority of people cannot hear the frequencies, their effect is to disorient and cause nausea and giddiness. The device has been tested on British soldiers at the army headquarters in Lisburn, Northern Ireland.

Injector Guns

These were initially developed for veterinary use, to facilitate the tranquilizing of large and dangerous animals from a safe distance. The round, which is actually a drug-filled syringe, is fired from a special gun—commonly air-powered. Upon impact, it injects the drug into the target. Much research into the application of such techniques for a police and military role has been done at Emory University, Georgia. The Palmer Chemical and Equipment Company, Georgia, has become particularly well known for its Cap-Chur range of related products.

Other Products

There are other developments, some of which are fanciful, some plain ridiculous, and some quite practical and worthy of use. They include an electrified water jet, which shoots two high-pressure water streams each carrying an opposing electrical charge. When the jets strike a human target, a painful electrical shock is produced. There is a cold brine projector—a water cannon that fires chilled brine; "banana peel"—a chemical that can be sprayed onto the ground making it too slippery to walk or drive on; and a photic driver, which produces a high-intensity flashing light of between ten and thirty cycles per second that disorients the target. This weapon has been used by the South African police, and versions of it are currently employed by some American police units. Last, but by no means least, there is continuing research into the "instant cocoon," which would be an adhesive chemical capable of literally sticking rioters together when sprayed with the substance from vehicles or helicopters.[6]

NOTES

1. Dick Lee and Colin Pratt, *Operation Julie* (London: W. H. Allen and Co.), 1978, pp. 117–118.

2. While the NSA probably does have the capability to thus monitor calls, one suspects that calls to and from certain parts of the world come under far greater scrutiny than others. At the time of writing, such areas would include Libya, Syria, and Iran.

3. *Securitech* catalog.

4. Declassified Central Intelligence Agency documents available under the Freedom of Information Act. See, for example, *MK ULTRA/Guided Animal Studies* material from the 1960s.

5. The most well known of these gases is CS (2-chlorobenzylidene nalonitrile). It was first synthesized in 1928 by Coroson and Stoughton. Its potential was tested at the Chemical Defence Experimental Establishment at Porton Down near Salisbury, England. The fact that the gas was a British discovery was kept quiet until 1968 when questions about its use were asked in the House of Commons. Information about CS and other chemicals was given to the United States in the early

sixties. The technique of putting CS into solution was perfected in 1965 in the United States, and many varieties of the substance are now available from private companies. For examples of the effects of CS gas above and beyond those expected, see *New Scientist,* 11 December 1975.

6. *Playboy,* September 1974.

14

Protection Measures for the Individual

As private individuals will remain targets of terrorism—primary or incidental—for the foreseeable future, it makes sense to lessen the risks that we face from this quarter in the normal course of our lives. Most defense techniques are common sense. By listing them here, we hope to provide a useful aide-memoire.

Risk assessment, *honest* risk assessment, is the cornerstone of any self-protection program. While bullet-resistant clothing, armor-plated vehicles, and a team of bodyguards may prove to be sensible and necessary measures for high-level potential targets—government employees, wealthy industrialists, and so on—such precautions are generally neither necessary nor practical.

We have seen in earlier chapters that the lower down the "status ladder" one falls, the fewer "official," organized security measures one benefits from. For example, other things being equal, the security for first-class passengers on an aircraft will be greater than that for their economy-class co-passengers. This greater "security" may, however, be only incidental, amounting to no more than such things as fewer passengers having to share an emergency exit, closer attention being paid to passengers during the journey, and closer scrutiny being given to ticket details.

The motivation for closer scrutiny of first-class tickets may be a desire on the part of the company to reduce financial losses due to counterfeiting, rather than an attempt to spot would-be terrorists. Antiterrorist considerations are likely to be in the background.

A stage will be reached when such incidental security is not enough. At these times, the safety of the individual depends entirely upon his or her own awareness and initiative. Avoidance techniques, rather than those of resistance and reaction, are of *primary* importance. In our own home, it is easy to imagine that our safety is inviolate. This is not true, of course, and some serious thought should be given to what is known as "hardening." It is not just inanimate objects that can be "hardened"; attitudes can be similarly treated.

Friends, relatives, and possibly neighbors of individuals at high risk should be made aware of the threat of terrorist aggression and asked to cooperate in a security program. They should not announce to others either the target's status or his/her impending travel arrangements. Such "announcements" are frequently made with the best of intentions, as in "Oh yes, we know someone who works for ---, he lives next door as a matter of fact." Seemingly innocent and harmless comments such as this can create serious problems for the potential target and other family members.

Senior directors and others of an obvious high-risk status may consider asking public-relations people employed by their company not to publicize details of their movements. Such movements could include attendance at a seminar, the opening of a new office building, and so on. Pre-event publicity in in-house magazines frequently finds its way into the national press. This can provide sufficient information for a terrorist group to plan and execute a successful kidnap operation.

Checking over mail before it is opened is a sensible policy. This applies especially to large and/or unusually shaped parcels. If in doubt, put the parcel in an unoccupied room and call for assistance.

If the family group of a high-risk indivudal includes children, arrange with their schools not to release a child to anyone but its parents or guardians under any circumstances. Further, a number should be left with school authorities at which the parents can be contacted if an attempt to secure the child's release during school hours is made. A common trick used by kidnappers of children is to approach the school and explain, for example, that there "has been an accident" involving the parents, who will thus not be able to collect them as usual.

A family "code" may be established, whereby the first person into the home performs some operation which is visible from the outside of the building (for example, opening a certain set of curtains or blinds, turning a light on or off in some particular room, etc.). Others approaching the property but *not* seeing the arranged signal can then assume that something is amiss. The same principle can be applied to work situations, of course. Keep knowledge of the signal limited to those who really need to know, and change it regularly.

With a view to reducing the odds of a successful kidnap against individuals within the confines of their own homes, a few simple and inexpensive measures can be taken.

Protection of Entrances

Installation of good-quality door and window locks is the first order of business. If the risk is high, consideration may be given to the installation of a metal window-shutter system. Shutters can be obtained which resemble an "antique" shutter design and thus will not require the owner to sacrifice the aesthetic quality of the property or to advertise his defenses. Good-quality, solid wood doors are infinitely preferable in this context to the "hollow" or "cavity" types. Door frames can be checked for strength and reinforced.

Alarm systems can be installed—the perimeter-type, protecting the area entrances; and structural, protecting the building itself. There are numerous types of alarms on the market, all of which have their pros and cons. Advice should be sought, therefore, from a competent alarm specialist, whose qualifications are endorsed by the police and/or a major trade body.

CCTV (closed-circuit television) systems are also available at a fraction of the price of just a few years ago. Such a system can be a powerful weapon in the cold-war world of terrorist versus target. Low-light systems are available, and these are good; but one should simultaneously install a security-lighting system. The video camera(s)—which should be aimed to cover all approach paths to the property entrances—should be connected to a video recorder enabling study to be made of recorded events at a later time.

THE "SECURE ROOM"

Setting up a secure area within the property is an extra measure that can be implemented quite inexpensively, should the individual feel that his target-status warrants it. The secure room may be any one which is already more inaccessible than others in the building. An upstairs bedroom, for example, which does not overlook any ground structures (as these can facilitate intruder access) is a good choice. The chosen room is reinforced in a conventional manner—with high-quality door and frame, locks and bolts (preferably not visible from the outside of the door), and window shutters. Important additions to the secure room into which the occupants should retreat in the event of an assault are a telephone extension, routed so that the line cannot be severed, and a master alarm control linked (as the other alarm circuits should be) to the police or an alarm-reaction team. An autodialer can be employed to call and transmit a prerecorded message to some designated number. The use in the secure room of one of the cellular telephone systems now available would nullify the risk of an intruder's cutting the conventional landline.

A detailed plan of the property and any existing security installations should be produced and kept with either a private security agency, the police, or a colleague. All information pertaining to the property should be included, even if it appears unimportant. Thus the plan should show not only entrances and exits, windows, floor plans, and the like, but also the location of air-conditioning units, ventilation bricks, sink overflow pipes, electricity boxes, etc. This detailed plan will prove invaluable to security-force personnel in a hostage or perpetrators-only siege situation.

Members of the household should be aware of the threat to the extent that they become familiar with basic security measures. Young children especially should become used to checking the CCTV system or (in a really basic situation) the door peephole before opening the door. If in any doubt as to the acceptability of the visitor, they should not open the door at all. A simple door-phone system can be installed, which enables the occupier to communicate with the visitor without having to open the door at all, or even approach it. Thus, if the caller cannot identify himself satisfactorily, the police can be called. "Official" callers should have in their possession an identity document of some type. The information from this can be noted and checked by phone. Very often, just the "threat" of this is enough to deter a would-be intruder who is pretending to be, for example, from the electric company, the water company, the target spouse's company, the child's school, etc.

THREAT BY TELEPHONE CALL: WHAT TO DO IF YOU GET ONE

It is of major importance that the whereabouts of family members are known at all times by as many other members of the household as possible. The phone number and/or address should be noted. If this is not possible—as may be the case if the individual is to visit some general area rather than a specific address—then check-calls should be arranged in advance. These simply require that the traveler calls home or the office at predetermined times. If one of these calls is missed, the authorities are immediately notified and the situation explained.

The "Threat Record"

A telephone tape recorder can be a good way of keeping a record of suspicious or out-and-out threatening calls. Where this technique is not employed, however, the following points should be borne in mind.

1. Never answer questions over the phone about the whereabouts or impending whereabouts of family members. If calls from individuals who do have a reason to ask and be informed of the whereabouts of friends or relatives (such as a spouse's employer, for example) are frequent, arrange a code word or comment in advance that the caller will always use to identify himself. It is all too easy for an aggressor to discover the name of the company for which a targeted individual works and then call the home of that individual under the guise of a company representative or colleague.

2. Keep a notepad by the phone and note down the following: the times of any suspicious calls made; whether the voice was male or female; whether the call was from a pay phone or a private number; any background noises heard (trains, heavy traffic, etc.); the acoustics of the call (was it echoey, muffled); and if the caller had an accent.

It is unlikely that many people will have the presence of mind to note down such details in the heat of an actual threatening call (which might be threatening an attack against an individual or property if some demand is not met; or harm to some individual who is, or is claimed to be, in captivity). But as an accurate "threat record" can be of tremendous help to any subsequently involved security agencies—police, military, private—the following example form may be copied and used to establish such a record with minimum effort.

Keeping such a document by the telephone will overcome to some extent the memory problems inevitably associated with such incidents. Although no amount of preparation will compensate for the shock of a threatening call, having at hand an aide-memoire of this type can prove invaluable once these initial emotions have subsided.

THREATENING-CALL RECORD

Date ________________ Time ________________

Phone booth/ private line ________________________

Male voice/ female voice ________________________

Accent Y/N

Kind of accent (if discernible) ____________________

Acoustics? i.e., muffled/ echoey/ very crackly ________

____

Background noise? Traffic/ trains/ voices/ machinery/ office noise/ animal sounds

____

Other ____

Specific target mentioned or hostage claimed to be held Y/N? Details

____

Inquiries made regarding whereabouts/ future movements?

____

Caller claimed to be? ______________________

Subsequently verified Y/N

If the caller claimed that a hostage was held, were you permitted to speak with him/her? Y/N

If yes, then details ______________________

____

If, at the time of completing this form, it was not possible to ascertain the true whereabouts of the supposed captive, do you believe that the individual to whom you spoke was, in fact, the individual in question? Y/N

If yes, then give reasons ______________________

____

Did the individual seem to be in pain? Y/N

Threats made or demands issued ______________________

____

Did the caller state or imply that the target's family/ friends/ colleagues were under surveillance and as a consequence would be jeopardizing their own and/ or the safety of the target if movements indicated an intention to contact the police? Y/N

Was any indication given as to the caller's ability to carry out this threat? Y/N

If yes, then details ______________________________

____

If checks fail to ascertain the exact whereabouts of the supposed captive or threatened target, the police (or other reaction agencies) will require the following information: a detailed description of the target, a recent photograph, details of his/her known movements since he/she was last seen; and details of his/her supposed movements since that time. A list of all the individual's friends, relatives, contacts, and business colleagues will also save a good deal of time and effort, as there always exists the possibility that the "captive" is not a captive at all, but rather cannot be contacted for some other reason.

Bluff Techniques for Ransom

Bluff techniques have successfully been used to obtain ransom payment. Such bluffs can only work, of course, if the true whereabouts of the target are not known to the recipient of the threat call. Thus, in the past, a bank manager has been fooled into handing over cash by a group that approached him and explained that they were holding his wife hostage. By dropping a few tidbits of accurate information about the wife (her usual movements, name of her hairdresser, etc.), the illusion created can be quite real. The only requirement is that the wife cannot be contacted. This is easily achieved by staging the operation to coincide with a visit by her to some place where she cannot be reached by phone. A more elaborate technique is to call the wife some considerable time before the operation is initiated and ask her a series of questions. Her responses are recorded and edited into some frightening phrase. "For God's sake, do what they ask" is extremely easy to piece together from any number of innocent comments.

TARGET-IDENTIFICATION PROFILE

Individuals who consider themselves to be high-risk targets may utilize the following form to establish their own identification profile for use by security agencies in the event of a successful kidnap assault. Individuals traveling to known terrorist trouble spots are advised to do this.

Profiles may be quickly established for all family members and left with the police or appropriate security force, who will then have valuable information with which to pursue their investigation. It would be ideal if a voice print is provided with this form. Precious time will be saved and attempts by "bandwagoning" groups to claim responsibility for the kidnap can be quickly discredited.

Name ______________________________

Date of Birth ______________________________

Height ______________ Weight ______________

Race ______________________________

Nicknames ______________________________

Distinguishing Marks ______________________________

Health Status ______________________________

Special Medical Requirements ______________________________

Blood Group ______________________________

Employer/occupational details ________________

School/teacher (if child profile) ______________

Hobbies ________________________________

Regularly attends? ________________________

Hair sample

Fingerprints

Photograph (front and profile)

Details pertaining to anyone with whom the individual is in regular contact, including addresses and phone numbers.

____

____

____

File this document, if possible, with a voice print of the individual.

TRAVEL

Careful consideration of the relationship between the government in an area one is to visit and one's own is an important first step in travel-risk assessment. It is apparent that this will have considerable bearing on the danger levels involved in the journey. Consideration must also be given to prevailing "grass roots" feelings, that is to say, the attitude of the indigenous population. This is frequently different from the official picture. Reading a wide cross-section of press reports can prove useful in this context.

Hostile attitudes in terrorists or extremists abroad—or at home for that matter—can be based on one's nationality, religious persuasion, or even skin color. The perceived links between an individual and the declared enemies of a terror group can be extremely tenuous. Simply having previously visited a country of which the government is regarded as an enemy can be enough justification for a fanatic to take an unfortunate traveler's life.

On occasion, the "terrorist" and "target" tables are turned unexpectedly with surprising consequences. Such was the case following the bombing of Libyan cities by the United States in April 1986. U.S. Air Force pilots carried out their mission with relative success and only minor losses. They evaded antiaircraft fire around the targets only to fly straight into a far heavier barrage of anti-Americanism upon their return to operational bases in the United Kingdom. The feverish enthusiasm which was evident among "peace" demonstrators as they screamed, "Get out American murderers," and hurled both abuse and rocks at the police and military personnel at hand, bore a direct parallel to similar scenes being transmitted from Libya. In Libya, we saw a humiliated and outraged people seeking revenge. In one interview, a Libyan citizen expressed the view that the local British expatriates community was now a justified target for such revenge. The Americans had staged the attack—at least in part—from English bases, and the British therefore themselves were culpable. The somewhat obvious fact that cluster bombs have no discriminatory sense and were, therefore, as likely to have killed or injured British personnel as those born locally seemed to have escaped him.

Following the same theme, an off-duty American serviceman, walking proudly through the center of London on the evening of the punitive strike, would have found himself a candidate for the "terrorist" label. A poor reward, some might say, from a people who only two short years previously had witnessed the unprovoked murder by Libyan terrorist-diplomats of a young, unarmed policewoman in the very same city.

It is worth mentioning at this point that, although media reports following the attack showed what could only be described as a massive anti-American backlash throughout Europe, one suspects that this was simply a continuation of the anti-Americanism usually found in European television news reports.

In an ITV/Harris poll, the results of which were broadcast on British television on April 16, 1986, it was shown that out of 1,056 people asked. "Was it right for the United States to bomb selected targets in Libya?" 59 percent answered "no." My own impression, on the other hand, based on conversations with British citizens of diverse backgrounds and character, is that a far higher percentage supported the move. The motivation for people with this viewpoint to proclaim their opinions loudly was not, apparently, as strong as for those who saw the attack as "an act of unprovoked aggression likely to lead to an increase in terrorism or a total nuclear war."

On the basis of this example, it is accurate to say that no broad assumptions can be made about who is likely to be seen as an enemy (and therefore a target). One should therefore assess the particular sociopolitical situation in the destination area at the time of making one's travel arrangements.

If an overseas visit is to be the first, some thought should be given to what occupation indicators, if any, need to be carried. In a hijack situation, for example, the worth as a target or hostage of an individual will often be determined by reference to the information provided by documents carried by that individual. It makes sense, therefore, to ensure that "provocative" descriptions–senior executive, journalist, civil servant, etc.–do not appear on any documents to be taken on the journey unless it cannot possibly be avoided.

The more alert chiefs of international companies whose executives must, by necessity, travel to, from, and through parts of the world in which terrorist activity is common, no longer have the arrival of such executives announced. Luggage tags carry no indication of the status of the traveler, and only the best protected or the most foolish of well-heeled individuals still insist on publicly announcing their worth as a target by demanding constant attention and traveling in an overly conspicuous manner. These same principles of discretion should be applied by any individual, since an "average" American, in some unstable and economically depressed parts of the world, quickly becomes a "rich Yankee imperialist."

Terrorist "Anniversary" Dates

Some thought can also be given to noting if any dates of significance to terrorists coincide with the outward or return journey, or the duration of one's stay. "Significant" in this context means dates that can sensibly be expected to provoke renewed or increased terrorist activity. The anniversaries of the death of a terror group martyr, or that of battles or coups from which a new regime connected in some way with a certain terror group emerged are examples of such dates.

April 1987 and subsequent years will, one suspects, see anniversary assaults against "imperialist targets" being perpetrated by factions connected with Khadafi. This will be true regardless of what the ultimate effects of the U.S. strike against Libya in April 1986 prove to be.

Air Travel

In the preceding chapter on aircraft and air terminals, we saw how important it is to choose a security-conscious carrier. If one single incident in recent times illustrates this point perfectly, it is the one that occurred on April 17, 1986, at Heathrow Airport in London. A female passenger was found to be carrying explosives in a specially prepared case. The significant point is that she had successfully passed through the normal terminal security checks, and her deadly baggage was only discovered by El Al security personnel during an additional preflight search. If the target in this instance had been the terminal staff and passengers at check-in or waiting areas, or an aircraft from a different carrier, then the terrorists would have scored another victory. Selecting secure carriers and terminals is not a simple matter, of course. Very often the choice is dictated by the destination and/or the required point of departure. However, if a traveler sees flaws in security that could be exploited by a terrorist, there is no reason at all why the flaws cannot be pointed out to a carrier or terminal representative. It has to be admitted, as the El Al incident proves, inconvenience *is* an acceptable price to pay for a higher standard.

Don't Travel Alone

In foreign countries or unstable local areas, traveling with others is far safer than traveling alone. This is especially so if the intention is to sightsee, as a normal consequence of such unplanned wanderings is to find oneself effectively lost and/or in a part of town which is home for the local "anti-imperialists." There is a far greater risk, of course, that in such areas the unwary traveler will be injured or killed by a nonideological thief. In any event, caution is warranted.

Trains

On trains or subways, choosing a compartment or car which is already partly occupied can effectively move one's status as a target lower down the "possibles" list. This is simply because in many cases, aggressors choose a target that can be attacked with as little risk of intervention or detection as possible. Measures such as this help counter possible threats only from a certain type of aggressor, of course. If a terrorist is intent on indiscriminate mass murder, a bomb or a burst of machine-gun fire can be extremely unselective. Other things being equal, however, it is somewhat safer to travel in the company of friendly locals (a family group including small children is to be preferred) than alone or in a small group of "foreigners." Traveling in a small group of "foreigners" is, on the other hand, slightly more secure than traveling alone. A simple rule of thumb applicable to the majority of situations is, *if in doubt, stay out.*

Changing One's Route

If it is necessary to attend business meetings or visit some seminar or other event regularly over the course of several days, it is an intelligent precaution to vary the route traveled to and from the event. This makes it difficult for a terrorist group to assess your probable position on any given day. This applies, of course, to any situation involving regular travel between two points. Even potential targets who consider their worth to a terror group negligible or nonexistent should ensure that some third party knows roughly what time they are due where, and what to do and who to contact if this appointment is missed.

Driving Tips

Driving in unknown areas where there is terrorist

activity should be limited to main roads, and at night, well-lighted areas. Hitchhikers should be ignored as should any pedestrian(s) who try to stop one's vehicle. Avoid, where possible, stopping to ask for directions, except at busy service areas, garages, and the like. Fake road accidents and operatives dressed as police personnel manning a "checkpoint" are two techniques which have been used in the past to bring a vehicular target to a standstill. Treating such situations with caution, then, is to be recommended. However, violently swerving and doing an about-turn to avoid a police check or a road worker with a stop sign is not being suggested here. Looking well ahead for such obstructions and making a detour (assuming this is possible, which, if it *is* a well-planned terrorist operation, will probably *not* be the case) as soon as the obstacle is seen would rate as more realistic. If one's vehicle is slowed or stopped by roadwork, traffic signals, or whatever, ensuring that a gear is selected which permits a rapid getaway should the need arise is a sensible policy. Similarly, driving with the doors locked and windows closed—particularly in the circumstances mentioned above—can buy valuable seconds if an aggressive move is forthcoming.

Individuals who are regularly chauffeured from point to point should not habitually sit in the same position in the vehicle. If it is usual for the driver to bring the vehicle to the home or office, for example, random changes should be introduced so that sometimes it arrives at the front door, sometimes at the back.

Taxi Tips

Occasionally a taxi should be taken instead. Even leaving the building itself via a different exit on a random basis can effectively throw any terrorist surveillance program into confusion.

Where a taxi is used, it should be ordered as near as possible to the time it is needed. Booking a considerable time in advance raises the possibility of a terrorist-sympathetic company employee tipping off relevant details. If a taxi must be chosen from a rank, it is wise *not* to select one which is occupied by anyone other than the driver. Share a cab only if you know other passengers.

Public Places

On occasion it can be prudent to avoid frequenting pavement cafes and other outdoor businesses that are close to foreign embassies, consuls, etc. This is because of the belief or knowledge of terrorists that the staff from such buildings spend some of their off-duty hours there. This makes them high-risk targets. The same can be said of any clubs or discos used by NATO military personnel.

Provocative opinions should not be expressed in cafés, clubs, shops, or bars; especially in bars in politically and socially unstable, volatile areas. Very often visitors to a foreign country—or even out-of-town visitors in an unfamiliar area—will be baited by aggressive supporters of some anti-American/anti-"imperialist" group. Rising to such bait—which might be a derogatory reference to one's government, apparent religious beliefs, or the prowess of an entire military force—must be avoided. As we have seen in earlier chapters, cash collections are sometimes made in bars and other meeting or drinking places on behalf of some extremist group. Often the collecting tin will be offered to new faces with a view to feeling them out. It is generally safest to make a token donation and then leave after finishing one's drink.

It is possible also that a stranger will be refused services in some places, simply on the strength of the political situation currently existing between his government and that of the area in which he finds himself. Even the relationship (past or current) between a third-party government and that of the customer can provoke this reaction. Many British holiday makers, for example, who happen to visit the "wrong" cafe or bar in Spain, still find themselves threatened with physical harm by pro-Argentinian locals who remain bitter about Britain's victory in the Falklands.

Should service be refused and abuse proferred in its place, it is wise to withdraw and avoid the area from then on. It must be said that by far the majority of Spanish citizens bear no real animosity toward the British with regard to the Falklands war. Pockets of anti-British sentiment can, of course, be found in that country, but no more than elsewhere.

The traveler should also be wary about reacting to shouts for "Mr. ———" in a public place. A terrorist hit team will have little choice but to assume that the individual who turns and looks in response to such a call is the Mr. ——— they are looking for, even if the response is prompted only by idle curiosity. It is also a sensible idea to avoid reacting automatically even when one's own name is called out. At the worst, this could mean that one *has* been targeted (for whatever reason) and one's probable location given to the hit team. At the best, it could be that the group is looking for someone else with the same surname. These cautionary words apply also to shouts from passing vehicles.

15

In Conclusion

It is the excusable opinion of many that a clear distinction exists between the supporters of and defenders against terrorism, the camps on either side representing "good" and "bad." This would be an ideal situation, of course, and one to be favored. It would, in essence, be a situation of declared war, in which enemies are apparent and their aims and intentions not subject to arbitrary interpretation. For the attacked, defense objectives would be easy to define and justify, and few qualms would be voiced as regards the tactics used to secure victory.

Unfortunately, so complex and far-reaching are the problems generated by peacetime terrorism, and, indeed, by the techniques used to counter them, that this black-and-white situation rarely, if ever, exists. Khadafi followers do not declare war on the United States but on "imperialism," and the Soviets denounce terrorism publicly while paying for its maintenance in many parts of the world. These variations in definition–terrorist vs. political activist–on an international level, plus the inevitable conflicts between personal sympathy and official duty, will continue to make for bent rules and blurred edges. The very nature of terrorist activity implies covert operation, deception, dishonesty, and immorality. To imagine that such an approach can be defeated without employing similar techniques is foolish. Little wonder then, that counter-terrorist agencies and operatives find themselves hailed as bastions of democracy one minute and condemned as inept and hopelessly corrupt the next. We can find an illustration of the techniques fundamental to countering terrorism and the associated problems in the following incidents. They are by no means unique. They should be considered typical.

In May 1981, a shipment of arms bound for the IRA in Dublin was found on-board an Aer Lingus jet at John F. Kennedy Airport in New York. The weapons had been hidden in cases marked "catering equipment," and were located by sniffer dogs. At that time, one Donald Donohue was the airport customs office chief, and on his staff was a special agent by the name of Stephen Rogers. In accordance with established practice, the airport office was offered support and liaison facilities from another customs-area group, which had established an impressive IRA data source and had up-to-the-minute information regarding IRA activities. The assistance was refused. In a subsequent interview, special agent Rogers justified this on the basis that the Public Prosecutor had asserted that the incident was not related in any way to other IRA activities in the area.[1]

A United States Treasury report, concerning among other things the activities and sympathies of Donohue and Rogers, reveals some illuminating facts. Firstly, Donohue was the close friend of an alleged IRA cell leader based in New York, whose primary activity is fundraising for the IRA. In June 1976, the name of this individual was placed on the Treasury list of top IRA suspects. This meant that he was subject to automatic search and interrogation upon arrival at any American port of entry. It was established in the Treasury report that Donohue had personally escorted his friend past the customs checks at JFK on numerous occasions, thereby allowing him to avoid controls.[2]

In November 1982, one George Harrison and four other Irish/Americans were charged with conspiring to smuggle ammunition, a flamethrower, and eighty-six machine guns to the IRA. In their defense, the accused admitted trying to get the arms out of the country to Ireland, but claimed that the CIA had sponsored the plan with a view to gaining end-user information. This claim was officially refuted, but the jury accepted it, and the five were acquitted. The jury later joined in the "victory" celebrations.[3] A few days later, the Treasury report states, Donald Donohue and other customs agents were seen drinking in a bar in New York. A toast was allegedly proposed by Donohue to George Harrison, which took the form of, "Let's drink to George, it's a great day for the Irish. Now they can get back to supplying the lads."[4]

In the summer of 1984, special agent Rogers traveled to Ireland and took part in a parade to commemorate the death of IRA hunger strikers. The march was organized by NORAID (Northern Ireland Aid, a North American IRA fundraising group) and the IRA political wing, Sinn Fein. Rogers denies being aware of this and claims that he was simply there in his capacity as a bagpipe player, a consequence of which is the regular opportunity to appear at a variety of fund-raising events. He denies even suspecting that members of Sinn Fein might also be members of the IRA proper, and sees nothing improper in a United States Customs agent attending such events.[5]

Former CIA operative Frank Terpil warrants inclusion in any work on terrorism, if only by virtue of the fact that he has aided and abetted the regimes of some of the most infamous practitioners of terrorism ever known. His inclusion in this particular section is justified by the fact that throughout his career he has been helped quite deliberately by the governments of the United States and Britain. Providing a free-lance service to the highest bidder, Terpil has supplied arms and related technology to such notable customers as Colonel

Khadafi of Libya, the former Shah of Iran, and Idi Amin of Uganda. It has also been reported that Terpil provided U.S. special-forces military personnel to train international terrorists in Libya; in a British television documentary, one such individual claimed to have received official leave of absence from his unit to participate in such training. Terpil and an associate, Edward Wilson, had lived in Britain during the 1970s, from where they coordinated their affairs with remarkably little interference from police or security services. This was possible thanks to Terpil's intelligence agency contacts, more specifically, one high-ranking special-branch officer and a security official, referred to in various reports only as "the baby-sitter." United States police officers, posing as Caribbean revolutionaries in the market for automatic weapons, eventually secured enough evidence against Terpil to lead to his arrest, conviction, and sentencing–fifty-three years. However, with the covert help of certain United States agencies, Terpil managed to flee the country before he could be incarcerated.[6]

In England in 1972, one Dennis Howard Marks was recruited by British Intelligence to penetrate an IRA arms-purchase-and-distribution network being financed by drug dealing. A known and active user and seller of drugs in his hometown, Marks fell into the role easily and soon established contact with international arms and drug dealers. At an early stage in the project, however, Marks engaged in various extracurricular activities, which alarmed his British controllers. Not the least of these was his close involvement with James McCann, an IRA gunrunner and drug dealer of some notoriety. This involvement led, according to British sources, to their ending their relationship with Marks. Marks, on the other hand, denies this emphatically.[7] In November 1973, Marks was arrested by British customs officers and charged with various drug offenses. The quantity of drugs involved, their street value, and the fact that Marks was a known international traveler would normally have guaranteed his immediate detention without bail. Yet bail *was* granted and Marks, of course, promptly fled the country.

He was to resurface in Britain officially seven years later when, in May 1980, he was again arrested for drug and passport offenses. It is known that in the interim period Marks had traveled widely—including in Britain—using fake documents. The value of the drugs Marks had been trying to import in this instance was approximately twenty million dollars. In November 1981, at his trial, he was found not guilty of the drug offenses and received a two-year sentence for passport irregularities. His defense has been based solely on his connection with, and work for, the British intelligence service. Although the prosecution and relevant agencies denied this, the jury was not entirely convinced. In February 1982, Marks was charged with the drug charges in relation to which he had been released on bail in 1973. He pleaded guilty and received an additional three-year sentence to run concurrently with the one he was already serving.[8] In view of the peculiar circumstances surrounding the Marks affair, which bear all the hallmarks of an intelligence operation, many people believe that he might still be a deep-cover agent for the British.

As for the others? I leave you to decide whether they would best be classified as friend or foe. A case of better the devil you know than the one you suspect, perhaps?

As we have seen, many terrorist actions—destructive and disruptive—resemble the actions one might find being employed by special-force units in an overt military campaign. These include sabotage, dissemination of propaganda, assassination of political and military leaders, and so on. Indeed, in many instances, the only additional factor required to change the status of such acts from terrorist to "legitimate" would be a declaration of war by the sponsors or perpetrators. We can conclude then, that in all but name, many acts of terrorism are acts of war by states that cannot afford—financially or politically—to issue such a declaration. Unfortunately, it is also impractical for many of the target regimes to react in a suitably aggressive manner. This is principally because the ensuing alignment and realignment of nations sympathetic to or opposed to the conflict would generate such serious international disruption as to effectively achieve the instigators' aims.

A concern of many, of course, is that, if in defending democratic society from terrorism the principles upon which it is founded are sacrificed, then the terrorists have won. While this might be true, there seems little point in advocating and supporting democratic principles if they can be nullified by a strategically placed lump of plastic explosive. The need then, to react with sufficient force and determination without falling into the trap of penalizing the innocent for the actions of others is paramount. The terrorist formula—democracy divided by terrorism equals totalitarianism—must be proven incorrect. The very fact that we do not always fight fire with fire is both our greatest strength and our most serious weakness. If any one thing is certain, it is that the terrorist of tomorrow will not be slow to exploit that weakness, in the name of existing causes, and those as yet unknown. Who, or what, will be *his* targets?

A tidal wave of anti-Americanism has swept through the Middle East in recent years, and it is from the fanatical groups in this part of the world that the greatest threat from terrorism emerges.

Syria is the home base of the most extreme of Palestinian groups. Although the Syrian government prefers denial to gloating, it is a major terrorist sponsor. But why should such regimes choose to support the actions of terrorists, and why should the terrorists involve the United States in their anti-Israeli struggle in the first place?

The majority of Arabs today see America as little more than the friend and ally of their perennial enemy, Israel. They know that terrorist/guerrilla offensives are the only way to score a victory over that enemy. The withdrawal of the Israeli forces from Lebanon was the result, as they see it, of terror tactics by Shi'ite groups. (The Shi'ite are a major Islamic sect. Certain Shi'ite elements, under the influence of Ayatollah Khomeini, have become vehemently anti-Western.) As Arabs see it, the United States was dealt a humiliating blow and pushed toward retreat from its ill-fated Mid-East involvement when Shi'ite factions destroyed the base of the Marine peacekeeping force in Beirut in October 1983. Two hundred and forty-one Marines died in the compound bombing, which was the largest non-nuclear explosion since World War II. The Islamic fundamentalist movement, of which certain Shi'ite groups form a part, is an extremely powerful force in today's Arab world. Its outlook entails total rejection of all Western values.

In Tripoli in 1984, a tripartite agreement was reached among the security services of Iran, Libya, and Syria. This agreement promised close cooperation in the war against the West as regards fake documents, identity papers, safe passage for terrorists, and so on. A principal beneficiary of this agreement is Abu Nidal.

Abu Nidal is an extremist Palestinian totally opposed to any negotiated settlement with the Israelis. The various Nidal terror groups are credited with over sixty terrorist operations. Apparently, the Nidal-Arafat split of 1974, following which former PLO member Nidal established his own Fatah group, is one to be taken at face value. His group has killed several PLO operatives loyal to Arafat, including Said Hammami in London in 1978. Abu Jihad (Khalil al-Wazir), Arafat's second in command and military commander of the PLO, is said to be high on Nidal's death list.

A primary pressure applied constantly to all Arab leaders comes from the Islamic fundamentalists. There is also a growing rejection of the West among many young, but nonfanatical Arabs. Such feelings are encouraged and supported by Soviet propaganda broadcasts to the area by Radio Moscow, which feed the disenchanted youth with a constant diet of biased, inflammatory material calculated to turn them away from the "imperialists." The Arab states do not, however, present a completely united front, and it was no coincidence that President Reagan's strike against Libya occurred at a time when the majority of Arab states thought as little of Khadafi as did Western leaders.

This friction existed because of Khadafi's support, in the Gulf war conflict, of non-Arabic Iran. His position opposes that of almost all the other states, which have backed Iraq. It is unlikely that retaliatory strikes by the United States against Libya will generate enough widespread support for Khadafi among these other Arab states to pose a serious threat to the U.S. or her allies. However, it cannot be denied that a lot of hard-earned goodwill has been lost.

Such is the dilemma faced by world leaders–to do nothing, or react decisively? In either case there can be no victory in the true sense of the word, but taking terror back to the terrorists in this case must be considered a positive step forward. The impunity which had hitherto been afforded to sponsors of terror thanks to overly liberal interpretations of international agreements governing the use of military force has been removed. A precedent has been set and while no one expects such action to stop the mad terrorist activity–indeed, retaliatory strikes are bound to provoke their own revenge attacks–at least those who would slice into the exposed jugular of a democratic, open society now know that such acts of ersatz warfare carry with them the risk–it is hoped, even the certainty–of swift retribution on a government-to-government level–the type traditionally provoked by more overt acts of aggression.

Terrorism will remain a weapon of "legitimate" and "illegitimate" regimes, groups, and organizations indefinitely. The "free West" also makes use, on a sporadic basis, of techniques which, when used today by groups holding some minority or internationally unrecognized status, are described as "terrorist." Indeed, a glance at the history books shows that acts of terror, truly horrific acts, perpetrated by state against state, and state against those that it perceives as a threat, have declined steadily over the years. Similarly, the acts of terrorism in recent years perpetrated *against* states and their representatives by ideologically motivated groups and mercenary anarchists, pale into relative insignificance when compared to those of the nineteenth and eighteenth centuries.

An uncommon ability to accept terrorism as the technique it is, is required by all concerned before its consequences can be properly understood. As has been implied before, condemning a terrorist act just because it *is* a terrorist act is a dangerous practice. Each act of terrorism must be analyzed in its context. To do this properly, it must be seen in terms of a much wider picture than that of the act and its victims.

In the definition portion of this book, we pointed to the difference in how an act of terrorism would be perceived if committed against the National Socialist regime of the Germany of 1939–1945 and if committed against the government of West Germany today. If we take the example a stage further and imagine that the target of that first attack had been one Adolf Hitler, and that the attack was successful, then one single act of murder/terrorism/assassination—call it what you will—would have saved the lives of countless thousands of innocent people and altered the entire face of post-1939 world history. Is it really so difficult to accept that others from time to time believe—albeit erroneously, perhaps—that a similar act against a different, present-day target might produce favorable consequences? And who, ultimately, should judge the morality of such decisions?

Denying the terrorist access to all vulnerable areas of a free society is an ambition which must be measured against the proportional loss of liberty that the true innocents within that society will face as a consequence.

As we have seen, the terrorist may be happy to settle for provoking just such an overreaction on the part of government. Although repressive measures are unlikely to drive the people *into* the terrorist's arms, they would almost certainly drive them *away* from the target regime—and this is in itself a terrorist victory.

It occurs to me also that denouncing violence, terror, war, and generally inculcating a desire for peace at any cost (as might seem to be a good way of combating terrorism) is a bad idea. We may find ourselves with a populace unwilling and/or unable to defend itself against the assaults of less pacifistic regimes. Far better, surely, is to work hard at encouraging societal loyalties and emphasizing the need for aggressive, violent—terroristic, even—strikes on our own behalf, be they retaliatory or preemptive, as and when the need arises. And arise it most certainly will. This assumes, of course, that those in a position to thus "educate" have a desire to do so.

In closing, consider the words of Thomas Jefferson: "The tree of liberty must be refreshed from time to time with the blood of patriots and tyrants. It is its natural manure."

NOTES

1. British television documentary discussing the Treasury report in question, shown nationally on 3 February 1985.
2. Ibid.
3. Ibid.
4. Ibid.
5. Ibid.
6. Ian Will, *The Big Brother Society* (London: Harrap, 1983), p. 84.
7. Ibid., p. 83.
8. Ibid., p. 84.

Appendix I

Potential Terrorist Targets

The following persons, companies, locations, and establishments have the potential of being targeted by terrorists. They are not listed in order of probability.

1. Air-terminal check-in, boarding, and loading areas of carriers based in or operating to and from an "enemy" area.
2. Aircraft operated by such carriers.
3. Government offices, especially those at which visas may be obtained in person by travelers to "enemy" areas. Also post office and telegraph offices, etc.
4. Offices of political groups, whose known views and aims oppose those of the terrorist group. Politicians and other personnel from such offices.
5. Clubs, bars, discos, etc., which are near to "enemy" military bases or are known to be frequented by military personnel.
6. Service clubs on military bases which are frequently opened to the public.
7. Companies known to supply or support declared enemies of the terror group. For example: construction companies which have been engaged in the construction or design of military bases or prisons for "political"/terrorist prisoners.
8. Companies with a subdivision based in, for exam-

ple, an area which is the subject of a nationalist dispute.

9. Persons employed by organizations to which the descriptions in "7" and "8" apply. The "status ladder" of those at risk is, broadly speaking (target choice will be determined as much by accessibility as status):
   a) owners
   b) senior directors
   c) senior management personnel
   d) middle and junior management personnel
   e) other employees
10. Military and police establishments—bases, stations, recruiting offices, etc.
11. Shops and stores selling products which are manufactured in or under license from an "enemy" regime, or products which in some other way pertain to "the cause."
12. Mass-transit systems.
13. Food sources.
14. Water supplies.
15. Power supplies.
16. Emergency reaction/repair personnel as they attempt to resolve problems created by assaults on 12, 13, 14, or 15.
17. Road systems—especially those with a high disruption potential (i.e., bridges). The probability of an attack against such targets increases if they lie on the route of nuclear-weapon-component-carrying transports, military exercise routes, produce/resource distribution networks, etc.
18. Transport known to be used by off-duty military personnel—returning from camps to home areas, for example, in chartered civilian transport.
19. Public displays and demonstrations by "enemy" military or police personnel, especially "soft" targets, such as military-band concerts.
20. Wealthy individuals, business persons and known

heirs to fortunes, especially those connected to some nationally or internationally known brand-name product or service.

21. Large public events, especially those involving international competition and media coverage: sports events, protest marches, etc.
22. Individuals who—although not wealthy or of high status—are mistaken as such because of outward appearances. Drivers of large, expensive rented cars, individuals wearing conspicuous jewelry, and so on.
23. Conferences at which terrorist-provocative matters (as determined by reference to current issues) are discussed.
24. Religious and political meetings and rallies.
25. Media offices/agencies, the output from which has been critical of the terrorist group's "cause" or methods. Propaganda "hijacks" or conventional attack.
26. Personnel from the above, especially journalists who have been fulfilling some foreign correspondent role in a "hot" area.
27. Any busy public areas at psychologically powerful times—Easter, Christmas, election day, etc.—or on any date which is significant to the terrorists.
28. Nationals from a third country in the company of citizens from a part of the world which is identified with a declared enemy of the terror group, such targets being "guilty by association."
29. Stores owned by individuals whose known religious persuasion is contrary to that of a terror group at least partly motivated by religious beliefs.
30. Seagoing vessels, especially passenger vessels, owned or operated by an individual or group whose known political or religious views are opposed to those of the terror group.
31. Banks. Overt assault or "withdrawal techniques" initiated with a view to disruption.

32. Schools and colleges at which the children of terrorist-provocative politicians, diplomats, or religious leaders are taught.
33. Hotels being used by visiting diplomats, religious leaders, or internationally known or wealthy individuals.
34. Industrial manufacturing premises.
35. Psychologically powerful areas where people traditionally gather to enjoy themselves—fairgrounds, sports arenas, holiday centers, etc.
36. Gas- and oil-distribution pipelines and related line stations.
37. "No-status" individuals, taken hostage in order to force a relative or close friend of the hostage to perform a specific act—for example, drive a vehicle containing explosives through a military checkpoint. This ploy is distinct from other "kidnaps" in which the aim is financial reward.
38. "No-status" individuals or family groups may be seized so that a specific property or location can be utilized for terrorist purposes. For example, at risk would be a family group whose home overlooks a military patrol route or the route to be used by politicians during a parade, or someone whose home or place of business can be used as a sniping point or observation point.
39. Socially important areas or objects may be occupied or threatened by a terrorist group seeking to use the psychological importance of the area or object as leverage for demands or simply to achieve a heightened level of publicity. Objects of high intrinsic value might also be used in this way. Examples of this category of target are major national monuments, internationally known symbolically important landmarks, valuable art collections, museums, etc.
40. Members of a royal family.
41. Communications centers and systems (telephone exchanges, microwave links, radio-relay stations).

42. Sewage and waste-disposal sites. Such raids can cause massive disruption and public reaction. The possibility of provoking disease epidemics exists here also.
43. Properties which lie on the routes to and from important military and political establishments. Such properties may be purchased legally by terror-group operatives or their surrogates. The properties can be used as staging points for attacks on important military or political figures. Admiral Carrero Blanco of Spain was killed in December 1973 by terrorists who had rented a basement room in a building along a route he was known to travel frequently. Group operatives dug out a tunnel twenty feet under the road and planted about a hundred and twenty pounds of explosives. The explosive material was divided into three separate charges, timed to explode at tenth-of-a-second intervals to match the speed of a moving vehicle. Sighting marks had been drawn on the wall of a building on the other side of the road. These were used to determine at what point the first charge should be triggered.
44. Nuclear establishments. These may be overtly attacked or be liable to theft of nuclear material by infiltration techniques. Such installations might also be subject to occupation. This would probably be accomplished using insiders, who have either been bribed or threatened with the death of a family member. Occupiers could threaten to bring about "meltdown" if certain demands were not met.
45. Retired police and military personnel and their families.
46. Prisons in which are held terrorist operatives, such attacks undertaken with a view to releasing the imprisoned terrorists.
47. Police vehicles which are carrying captured terrorists, to a court hearing, for example. Either with

a view to releasing the terrorists, or ensuring their silence.

48. Passport and birth/death registry offices, and similar departments from which important documents are issued. Either overt attacks made with a view to theft or infiltration techniques.
49. Civil nuclear facilities, employees from such facilities, their families.
50. Nuclear test sites, especially "abandoned" ones, targeted by terrorist groups with a view to the collection of contaminated material for use in bluff projects or re-distribution/contamination projects. Many of the early test sites are easily accessible to unauthorized personnel.

Appendix II

Mail-Bomb Recognition

While the chances of an "ordinary" citizen receiving, without provocation, some type of terrorist device in the mail are slim, the possibility should not be dismissed. We have seen throughout this study that a terrorist's definition of a "fair target" can be very different from that of his victim or third-party commentators. Thus an action as innocent as visiting the local supermarket can result in frightening consequences if the store happens to be owned or run by some individual or group regarded by terrorists as the enemy. A basic example is that of a Palestinian or other Arab group that is targeting Jewish business concerns. A member of the local operational cell secures employment at one such business—the supermarket—and uses this position to set up a list of regular customers. If goods are delivered—as is quite common—the operative would be able to collate names, addresses, and suitable attack times. Rather than risk compromising their infiltrator, the group might decide to initiate a mail-bomb campaign against these customers anonymously.

(Incidentally, planting explosives devices among the items for sale in stores and supermarkets is by no means unknown. In June 1977, an Irish housewife inadvertently purchased a terrorist incendiary along with her week's shopping. The device, hidden in one of the items, went off in a child's bedroom. Fortunately, in this instance there were no injuries and little damage.)

The basic letter-bomb is relatively easy to recognize. Designs vary and it is not possible to say a letter-bomb looks like thus-and-such. Nevertheless, there are some common denominators which should enable the cautious recipient to discern whether or not a letter or parcel is an explosive device.

Of fundamental importance here is constant awareness. One should never fall into the trap of opening mail automatically. One should make at least a cursory inspection. Where does the postmark show the piece of mail to be from? Has it been sent by someone we know? Are we expecting a letter/parcel from someone or some organization in the area indicated by the postmark? These are the basic questions that one should consider before opening any article of mail.

Any mistakes or oddities in the spelling of the name or address should cause suspicion, especially if a familiar sender's name and address are shown on the envelope or wrapping. A known terrorist trick is to use the names of a target's friends and acquaintances or those of official departments associated with him or her to enhance the impression of the item's authenticity.

The letter-type device is likely to be quite large, at least the size of a standard business envelope in length and width, and have a stiff feel to it. The object will be more rigid than would folded paper sheets giving the same size. It will also be heavier. The actual thickness of the envelope will be determined by the type and quantity of explosive material employed. "Plastic" explosive devices may be a quarter of an inch thick or thicker, but if the device is hidden inside a book, for example, this thickness will be less obvious. If the letter has traveled via the mail, it can be *relatively* safely assumed that it is not designed to detonate until opened. This fact cannot be relied upon, however, and handling should therefore be kept to a minimum.

Any smell from the package should arouse suspicion. Some explosives have peculiar smells. It is often said that plastic explosives smell like marzipan. Some type of chemical or perfume may be used in an effort to conceal this giveaway smell, however; or the material may be well sealed and surrounded by an odor-absorbing substance, such as activated charcoal. The envelope paper may also show signs of grease or oil. This can indicate a poorly covered "sweating" explosive, and should arouse suspicion.

An odd variant of the letter-bomb was used in 1972 against a Dutch-Jewish businessman, who received a letter postmarked Karlsruhe (West Germany). He became suspicious and notified the police. Subsequent investigation proved the letter not to be a bomb, but rather a gas device containing forty grams of powdered cyanide. Upon exposure to oxygen in the air, the material would have reacted chemically and produced deadly cyanide gas.[1]

SUMMARY OF PRECAUTIONS

1. Check postmark and details of name and address. If your suspicions are not aroused, you may proceed. If they are, call police.

2. Check gently for elasticity. If the size and shape of the package implies a book or papers, but a bend test indicates a lack of "springiness" (as you would find in bending plasticene, for example), treat the package with caution. Suspicious? No, proceed. Yes, call the police.

3. Check the envelope for greasy marks and odors. Suspicious? No, proceed. Yes, call the police.

4. Check the package with a small metal detector. While not all devices will include a metallic component, many will, and the presence of metal in any significant quantity (enough to trigger a cheap, hand-held detector) should cause suspicion. This is *especially* true if the package also satisfies some of the other "suspicion conditions." Suspicious? No, proceed. Yes, call the police.

5. Open the package or envelope carefully. In the case of the latter, cut off a strip from the top of the envelope and, with the item at arm's length, shake out the contents. If the contents prove to be another sealed or closed package–a card folder, for example, or a hardback book, the covers of which have been secured with tape or an elastic band; *and* if no such item is expected–suspicion is called for and the police or security forces should be notified. Secured covers could indicate that some type of spring-action detonation system is being kept "safe" for as long as the covers are together. It might also be that an electrical circuit is thus being kept shorted. When the covers are opened, the spring can trip or the circuit operate; either condition can be used to detonate a bomb or incendiary. The friction-tape technique may also be used on both outer or inner covers. This tape produces sparks when torn apart and can ignite some incendiary mixtures.

It is obvious that the point at which a letter or parcel becomes suspicious will depend on the lifestyle and status of the individual. In the gas-bomb example, the Jewish businessman had a good reason to suspect that the letter was what it seemed to be. If it had borne a local postmark and the name of a known Jewish group, however, one suspects that he might not have reacted with such caution. While the security forces would rather be asked to deal with a dozen false alarms than allow one actual incident (assuming the false alarms are not the product of malicious pre-meditation, of course), they are unlikely to rate highly the individual who calls in a bomb alert on the strength of receiving an unexpected letter which happened to sport grease marks. *Intelligent* context-sensitive interpretation of the measures suggested here is called for. The outspoken politician is far more likely to receive a mail bomb than Mr. Brown the painter and decorator; unless, of course, Mr. Brown happens to be undertaking an important job for some known individual or group inimical to some terrorists! Thus it is possible to sensibly assess the odds for and against an item being a terrorist device *only* in the light of attendant situations.

Although a mail bomb may be sent at any time, there are certain times that merit increased caution. These are any times shortly after a terrorist group has suffered some defeat and/or threatened a renewal of activity with diversification of targets. Other times for caution are those—such as Christmas, birthdays, anniversaries—when unexpected letters and parcels will not generate a high degree of suspicion. On such occasions it is all too easy to try to identify the origin of a letter or parcel in a vein such as, "I'll bet it's from old so-and-so." Bright and cheerful wrapping, a card with friendly greetings—all such trappings of celebratory occasions only help to disguise further the true nature of the item.

Some identification problems can be overcome by arranging with friends, relatives, and business colleagues to include on the outside of the letter or parcel some simple agreed-upon code or sign. There can never be a guarantee that some suitably motivated group or individual will not learn of and use these codes—if only by the interception and duplication of a legitimate letter. Nevertheless, such codes will tend to reduce the chances of being very unpleasantly deceived.

NOTES

1. Christopher Dobson and Ronald Payne, *The Weapons of Terror* (London: Macmillan, 1979), p. 123.

Appendix III

Selected Terrorist Groups

AD
Action Directe

Principal area of operations: France, Europe

Objectives: AD was established in May 1979 in France by Jean-Marc Rouillan and Nathalie Menignon. In 1980 these two leaders were arrested but later pardoned by the French authorities. It is an anti-Jewish, anti-NATO group.

Size: The group is believed to be small—around a dozen active members—but it has undertaken several campaigns of assassination and bombing.

Principal targets: Jewish businessmen and business properties, NATO personnel and establishments, and individuals perceived by the group to be linked in some way with these primary targets.

Links: Other European anti-NATO terror groups.

Status: Active.

ALF
Arab Liberation Front

Principal area of operations: Middle East, Europe

Objectives: The ALF was formed in 1969 with substantial Iraqi support as an opposition movement to the Syrian-backed Al-Saiqa. It is a member of the extremist Palestinian Rejectionist Front, a group that totally opposes any negotiated settlement of the Palestinian problem. The ALF is currently based in Iraq.

Principal targets: Any groups or individuals perceived by the ALF as being supportive of the Israeli regime.

Links: Other Arab terror groups, notably the more militant ones.

Status: Active.

ALN
Acao Libertadora Nacional

Principal area of operations: Brazil

Objectives: This was a left-wing terrorist group active in Brazil in the 1960s and early 1970s. One of several such groups, the ALN–whose most famous leader was Carlos Marighella, author of *Minimanual of the Urban Guerrilla* (a text on urban terrorism)–failed to achieve their goal of "people's power" because of a lack of total popular support and the violent reaction of the Brazilian security forces. Marighella was shot dead in a police ambush in November 1969, as was his successor Camara Ferreira in October 1970.

Principal targets: Any groups or individuals perceived as being supportive of the incumbent regime or "imperialism."

Links: Other Brazilian terror groups and other left-wing Latin American groups.

Status: Defunct.

ANC
African National Congress

Principal area of operations: Southern Africa

Objectives: The ANC was established as a political party in 1912. Any claims the organization may make that it is not a terrorist group were proven beyond doubt to be vacuous in 1984 when bombs were planted in a number of South African city center areas, causing injury to both black and white victims.

ANC operatives have also intimidated or killed blacks whom they claimed were supportive of the

South African government.

Principal targets: Black government "sympathizers," and any group or individual perceived as being supportive of the South African government and apartheid. This group is essentially communist in doctrine.

Links: The Soviet government, other Communist groups internationally. The ANC has camps and bases in Zimbabwe, Botswana, and Mozambique. Many of its operatives receive training in guerrilla warfare from Soviet/Eastern Bloc "advisors."

Status: Active.

Angry Brigade

Principal area of operations: England

Objectives: This group was one of several "new left" (wing) groups which emerged from the student unrest in the 1960s. Having elements in common with its French, German, and Italian counterparts, the Angry Brigade borrowed various leftist ideologies as–and when–such ideologies suited a particular action. The group was essentially anti-"imperialist" and anarchical in profile.

Principle targets: "Establishment" targets, mostly buildings.

Links: Baader-Meinhof, Red Brigade(s), and other left-wing movements.

Status: Defunct/inactive.

April 19 Movement (M19)

Principal area of operations: Colombia

Objectives: Destabilization/overthrow of the existing Colombian regime. This is a right-wing group which engages not only in terrorist operations but also in guerrilla actions in support of the Colombian Popular Liberation Army.

Elements of M19 have staged several attacks including the bombing of the Colombian Communist Party headquarters and the murder of at least two prominent left-wing leaders. One of the group's more spectacular actions was the seizure of an entire town of some 35,000 people which they held for almost eight hours. At the time of writing, M19 continues to threaten to kidnap executives of foreign corporations.

Links: Colombia Popular Liberation Army, Colombia Revolutionary Armed Forces.

Status: Active.

ARC
Action pour la Renaissance de la Corse

Principal area of operations: Corsica. Some attacks against French mainland targets.

Objectives: Corsican self-determination. This is a nationalist group desirous of control of the island's resources by Corsican nationals. The group has been successful in persuading the French government to withdraw Légion étrangère training facilities from the island.

Links: Other Corsican nationalist groups and (some sources claim) Libya.

Status: Active.

ASALA
Armenian Secret Army for the Liberation of Armenia

Principal area of operations: Europe, U.S.A.

Objectives: The establishment of an independent Armenian state. The ASALA propaganda material explains that the Turks have for many years repressed and exploited the Armenian people, denying them the right to establish and enjoy their own culture. It is also claimed that in the years 1915/1916, the Turks massacred some 1.5 million Armenians. The group was formed in Beirut in 1975.

Principal targets: Turkish diplomats serving abroad and other groups or individuals perceived as being supportive of the Turkish government.

Links: Other pro-Armenian groups in Turkey, Europe,

and the United States.
Status: Active.

Baader-Meinhof

Principal area of operations: Western Germany, Europe
Objectives: Formed originally as RAF (Red Army Faction) in the 1960s, the group eventually adopted the name of its two most famous leaders, Andreas Baader and Ulrike Meinhof. Both individuals were captured by West German security forces and ultimately committed suicide in prison. The group was effectively smashed in the early 1970s. More recently, reports that the group has been reformed have emerged, and it is believed that the Baader-Meinhof/Red Army Faction terrorist cells now form part of the European anti-NATO alliance.
Principal targets (currently): NATO personnel and establishments, nuclear facilities, and personnel employed by nuclear authorities.
Links: Other anti-NATO terrorist groups, PLO, IRA, ETA, and Cuban and Salvadoran groups.
Status: Active.

Black June

Principal area of operations: Middle East, Europe, India
Objectives: This group was formed in 1976 by "Abu Nidal," the former partner of Yasser Arafat who split from the mainstream PLO to further his extreme views. Nidal–who operates under a variety of banners–is not only dedicated to the destruction of the Israeli regime and the restoration of a Palestinian homeland, but favors the annihilation of Arafat and the rest of the current, "moderate" PLO leadership.
Principal targets: Western diplomats and businessmen, and anyone perceived as not being sympathetic to the Palestinian cause or who is supportive of Israel.
Links: Other Palestinian groups and the governments of Libya, Syria, and Iraq.
Status: Active.

Black September

Principal area of operations: Middle East, Europe

Objectives: The name of this "group" is taken from a month in 1970 during which the Jordanian government fought and defeated the Palestinian terrorist groups based in that country. Some seven thousand Palestinians died in the fighting. "Black September" is known to be one of the many aliases used by terror groups controlled by "Abu Nidal" when targeting certain individuals and organizations. It is an anti-Israeli, pro-Palestinian group.

Principal targets: Israeli and Western businessmen and political figures, and anyone perceived as being supportive of the Israelis.

Links: Other Palestinian groups and the governments of Iraq, Syria, and Libya.

Status: Active.

BR
Brigate Rosse
(Red Brigade)

Principal area of operations: Europe

Objectives: This organization was formed in 1969 from various Italian "anti-imperialist" types, many of whom attended the University of Trento. At that time, the overriding motivation behind its actions was U.S. involvement in Vietnam. The violence perpetrated by this now-large group continued to escalate. In March 1978, the group kidnapped and eventually murdered Christian Democratic party leader Aldo Moro. The Italian security forces consequently arrested more than two thousand suspected terrorists and terrorist sympathizers.

Following the release by the group of kidnapped American General James Dozier in December 1981, the BR cells went underground and little was heard of them until they claimed responsibility for the murder of American Leamon Hunt, the director of the multinational peacekeeping force in the Sinai. The group is currently part of the European anti-NATO terrorist alliance.

Principal targets: American businessmen and diplomats, NATO personnel and establishments, and anyone perceived as being an "imperialist."

Links: Other terror groups with left-wing leanings in Europe, the PFLP, IRA, and ETA.

Status: Active.

CCC
Cellules Communistes Combattantes (Fighting Communist Cells)

Principal area of operations: Belgium, Europe

Objectives: This group announced its existence in October 1984 with an attack on Litton Data Systems, Belgium. Since that time the group has perpetrated several murders and bombings, and is believed to be led by one Pierre Carrette. Carrette is a former AD (Action Directe) operative who took refuge in Belgium in 1981.

Principal targets: NATO personnel and establishments, other companies and their employees and owners who are believed by the group to be helping in some fashion to maintain NATO.

Links: CCC is a member (since 1984) of the anti-NATO alliance of terrorist groups.

Status: Active.

Christian Phalange

Principal area of operations: Middle East

Objectives: The Christian Phalange (also known as the Christian Militia) was formed before World War II in opposition to the growing Muslim influence in Lebanon (a traditionally Christian country).

The Christian Phalange is well funded—often by the Israelis, it is claimed—and has fought against the PLO in two civil wars and during the Israeli offensive in Lebanon.

Principal targets: PLO factions.

Links: Governments of Lebanon and Israel, and other anti-PLO groups.

Status: Active.

CSAMEP
Committee of Solidarity with Arab and Middle Eastern Prisoners

Principal area of operations: France, Europe

Objectives: This group is dedicated to securing the release of Arab terrorist prisoners held in various European countries, most notably France.

Principal targets: The government and private citizens of any country which is holding Arab/Arab-sympathetic terrorist prisoners.

Links: Arab terror groups worldwide to varying degrees.

Status: Active.

DFLP
Democratic Front for the Liberation of Palestine

Principal area of operations: Middle East

Objectives: This is another anti-Israeli, pro-Palestinian movement. The DFLP is a PFLP (Popular Front for the Liberation of Palestine) breakaway group, formed in 1969 by Naif Hawatmeh and others. These individuals believed that political dialogue, rather than military force, was the key to resolving the Palestinian homeland problem. The DFLP is an extremely political movement which maintains close links with the Soviet Union and Communist China. Although the DFLP is a PFLP breakaway, the two groups do undertake occasional joint actions.

Principal targets: Israeli personnel.

Links: Other Palestinian groups. The governments of the Soviet Union, China, Iraq, Syria, and Tunisia. It also has bases in the Sudan.

Status: Active.

ELN
Ejercito de Liberacion Nacional

Principal area of operations: Bolivia, Colombia, Peru

Objectives: This was one of a number of left-wing groups operating in Latin America during the 1960s and early 70s. It was one of the groups which founded the Junta of Revolutionary Coordination along with the Chilean MIR, the Argentinian ERP, and the Tupamaros.

Principal targets: Government establishments and politicians, and Latin American diplomats serving in Europe.

Links: Other Latin American terror groups with leftist policies.

Status: Defunct/inactive, some elements operational under different banners.

EOKA
Ethniki Organosis Kypriakou Agoniston (National Organization of Cypriot Fighters)

Principal area of operations: Cyprus

Objectives: This organization was active in postwar Cyprus. Its primary purpose was to drive the British occupying forces out of the country. Isolated incidents of terror—directed mainly against the British—escalated into mass rioting which, by 1956, had become commonplace. The presence of Turkish citizens in the operational areas only served to complicate matters.

Principal targets: British military personnel and civilian "sympathizers."

Links: Other anti-British movements of the period.

Status: Defunct.

ERP
Ejercito Revolucionario del Pueblo

Principal area of operations: Argentina, El Salvador

Objectives: The ERP was established in Argentina with the purpose of wiping aside the continual ideological discourse of the Latin American left and replacing it with action. A left-wing group of sorts, the ERP decried the "hair-splitting" of their Trotskyist colleagues. The vagueness of their ideologies may, of course, have been partly tactical. The organization earned itself millions of dollars via bank robbery and ransom through kidnapping.

The ERP's factional groups occasionally staged assaults against military camps, but these were never completely successful.

Principal targets: Latin American diplomats, trade union leaders, military personnel, and wealthy industrialists.

Links: Other leftist Latin American groups.

Status: Inactive/defunct; some elements operational under different banners.

ETA
Euskadi ta Askatasuna
(Freedom for the Basque Homeland)

Principal area of operations: Spain

Objectives: Formed in 1959, this organization seeks independence from Spanish rule for the Basque people living in Northern Spain. The group has had some success in forcing concessions from the Spanish government. Much like the IRA – with whom it is known to have regular contact–the ETA has split into several factions. The most violent of these are ETA-M and the Autonomous Commandos.

Principal targets: Spanish politicians and members of anti-Basque groups.

Links: Other Basque separatist groups, the IRA, PLO, FLNC, AD, BR, FP25, RAF, CCC, and Polisario.

Status: Active.

FALN
Fuerzas Armadas de Liberacion Nacional

Principal area of operations: Venezuela, Puerto Rico

Objectives: This group was most active in the late 1960s and early 70s. It was leftist in outlook and one of several similar Puerto Rican movements which objected to Puerto Rico's growing links with the U.S.

Principal targets: "Imperialist" targets, policemen, and public offices–including some attacks on buildings and personnel in the U.S.

Links: Other anti-American, left-wing groups of the period.

Status: Defunct/inactive; some elements operational under different banners.

FAR
Fuerzas Armadas Revolucionarias

Principal area of operations: Argentina

Objectives: This was a left-wing, Peronist group active in the late 1960s and early 70s. It was part of the massive Latin American terrorist emergence of the period.

Principal targets: Banks, "imperialist" targets, wealthy industrialists, and government offices and personnel.

Links: Other anti-American, left-wing movements of the period.

Status: Defunct/inactive; some elements operational under different banners.

FARC
Fuerzas Armadas Revolucionarias Colombias

Principal area of operations: Colombia

Objectives: This group was originally formed in 1966. Its activities escalated during the 70s, during which time its principal tactic was to kidnap for money. By the early 80s, the group had established itself as a private army protecting cocaine growers. In 1984, the group agreed to a government-offered amnesty which, among other incentives, included the promise of government jobs for some of the terrorists. For the most part, the group has honored its part of the bargain.

Principal targets: At the time of writing, these would seem to be anyone threatening to interfere with the group's highly profitable cocaine protection rackets.

The group was originally Communist oriented.
Links: Other Colombian guerrilla/terrorist groups.
Status: Active.

Fatah (Al-Fatah)
(Harakat al-Tahrir al-Watani al-Filistini)

Principal area of operations: Middle East/International
Objectives: This organization, whose official title can be translated as meaning the Palestine National Liberation Movement, was the first military group to fight for the Palestinian cause. It became universally known in the late 1960s when its leader, Yasser Arafat, was elected chairman of the PLO Executive Committee. Despite Arafat's public denouncement of terrorism when speaking on behalf of the PLO, Al-Fatah elements frequently undertake terrorist actions. In common with other Palestinian groups, this fact is concealed via the adoption of operational names which differ from the actual perpetrators.
Principal targets: Perceived enemies of the Palestinian movement.
Links: Other Palestinian groups.

Fatah Revolutionary Council

Principal area of operations: Europe, Middle East
Objectives: This is a hard-line Palestinian liberation group, led by Abu Nidal. It is totally opposed to any compromise or peace initiative with Israel. It was this group that perpetrated the vicious airport assaults at Rome and Vienna in December 1985.
Links: The governments of Libya, Iran, and Syria. "Abu Nidal" is a long-established figure in the world of Palestinian terrorism, and has established numerous factions over the years. For some time, Nidal was supported by Iraq, but more recently (1980) has established an operations base in Damascus. (See PLO.) Abu Nidal is believed to be a nom de guerre for Sabri al-Bana.
Status: Active.

FLQ
Front de Liberation du Quebec

Principal area of operations: Canada

Objectives: This is essentially a nationalist/separatist group which seeks to establish some kind of independence from the Canadian authorities for the French-speaking citizens of Quebec province. It was established in 1963 and has undertaken various actions since that date. The group is leftist oriented.

Principal targets: Government ministers and various Canadian-controlled targets.

Links: IRA, ETA, BR, AD, and others.

Status: Active under this and other operational names.

FP25
Forcas Populares do 25 Abril

Principal area of operations: Portugal, Europe

Objectives: This group was formed in Portugal in 1980. Though a small group, it has carried out several attacks against civilian and military targets. Essentially an anti-NATO, anti-"imperialist" group, it has carried out attacks against British targets in Portugal in support of the IRA.

Principal targets: NATO installations and personnel, civilian contractors who work—directly or indirectly—for NATO, and other groups and individuals specified by other terror groups. This group is also a member of the anti-NATO terrorist alliance.

Links: Other anti-NATO factions in Europe and elsewhere.

Status: Active.

IMRO
Inner Macedonian Revolutionary Organization

Principal area of operations: Macedonia, Bulgaria

Objectives: Initially a nineteenth-century propaganda organization, IMRO developed into a fully fledged terrorist group/guerrilla army. Attempts at provoking mass insurrection, however, failed. The primary objective of the organization was to secure independence for Macedonia from Turkey. Early efforts failed to achieve this goal, and in 1912/1913 Macedonia was redistributed among the governments of Serbia, Bulgaria, and Greece. IMRO continued its fight from Bulgaria and staged some attacks against Yugoslavia. Internecine fighting ensured that no properly coordinated assault against the oppressor regimes could be staged and no victory in the true sense achieved.

Principal targets: Various targets perceived as "enemy" by various IMRO factions.

Links: Other separatist/nationalist movements of the period and the Bulgarian government (which used IMRO operatives for its own ends to some extent).

Status: Defunct.

INLA
Irish National Liberation Army

Principal area of operations: Northern Ireland, Great Britain (mainland)

Objectives: This is an IRA breakaway group, formed in the late 1970s. It is a vicious and brutal organization whose members are violently committed to the expulsion of British forces from Ulster (Northern Ireland). It is also a Marxist/Leninist group whose political aspirations amount to the establishment of a united socialist Ireland.

Principal targets: British military personnel and politicians, members of Protestant groups, anyone perceived by the group as being supportive of the British regime in Ireland, businessmen, members of the Irish police force–and their friends and relatives.

Links: Other Catholic terror groups and almost all of the left-wing international terror groups.

Status: Active.

IRA
Irish Republican Army
(and factions)

Principal area of operations: Northern Ireland (Ulster), the British mainland.

Objectives: Reunification of the twenty-six counties of southern Ireland (Eire) with the six counties of the North still under British rule.

History: The history of violence in Ireland is a long one. In Elizabethan times, small Irish groups or "clans" fought to resist English colonizers around the "Pale"—the area around Dublin.

By the eighteenth century, secret societies known as "Defenders" (Protestant groups) and "Whiteboys" (Catholics) fought each other over religious issues and land rights. The "war of independence" against British control in 1919–1921 won back the southern counties.

After sporadic campaigns failed to achieve their aims, the minority Catholic population in the North embarked on a series of "civil rights" programs in the late 1960s. Many Protestants viewed this as a threat and reacted aggressively to Catholic marches and demonstrations. Angry verbal exchanges grew into street battles, and these soon developed into overt warfare between the sectarian groups.

The RUC (Royal Ulster Constabulary) and, in the early days, the "B" Specials," found themselves unable to cope with the escalating violence. In August 1969, the British regular Army was moved into the North as a peace-keeping force.

It was inevitable that this "occupation" would provoke renewed activity from the Irish nationalist groups. The IRA proper had been undergoing reorganization since 1964, which was the time that Marxist computer scientist Roy Johnson was appointed to the IRA Army Council. By 1969, several hundred old hands had left or been ousted from the organization, which had now taken a pace or three to the left.

Many of those members whose primary concern was military action formed the PIRA, the Provisional Irish Republican Army (the "Provos"), initially as the military wing of Provisional Sinn Fein (We, Ourselves). A further split occurred in 1974, when a small group of extremists formed the INLA, the Irish National Liberation Army. This is the group that killed Conservative spokesman for Ulster, Airey Neave, with a car bomb in the House of Commons parking lot in April 1979. This was the first time that a "dual-trigger" device had been used in England. Its use fueled speculation that the Irish terrorists were cooperating closely with other groups–the PLO and the Red Brigade had used such devices frequently.

Links: The IRA has received covert support and overt expressions of sympathy from the Soviet Union for the Irish "just cause" since the 1920s. In the 50s, links between the Irish terrorists and the EOKA (National Organization for Cyprus Fighters), who were fighting against the British in Cyprus, were established. Firm links also exist between the IRA and factions and the Breton Separatists, the PLO, Syrian and Libyan groups, and the FLQ (Front de Liberation Quebequois). Soviet-made SA-7 (Strela) missiles have been smuggled into Ireland via Belgium in Libyan diplomatic baggage. (Such baggage, because of international agreements, cannot be searched.)

Omnipol, an armament factory in Czechoslovakia under the control of East-Bloc intelligence elements, shipped rifles, antitank mines, explosives, and various small arms direct to the Provos in October 1971. However, the shipment was intercepted at Schiphol Airport in Amsterdam. IRA operatives have been trained in Jordan and other Middle East countries by PLO factions. In 1973, a PLO spokesman in Beirut announced "joint military operations on British territory against Zionist organizations." This statement was made as part of a confirmation of solidarity between the PLO and the IRA. KGB and DGI (Cuban) links are also well established. The Irish terror groups benefit greatly from cash donations and gifts of weaponry and other equipment, which regularly find their way from sympathizers in North America to the "freedom fighters" in Londonderry and Belfast. It is widely accepted that a degree of "unofficial-official" sympathy exists for the Irish nationalist movement in the United States, and a "blind eye" has been turned on more than one occasion to the activities of IRA gun runners.

Irgun
Irgun Zvai Leumi

Principal area of operations: British Mandatory Palestine
Objectives: The primary objective of this organization was the establishment of an Israeli homeland independent from British control. The group was active prior to and following World War II.
Principal targets: British occupying forces and "sympathizers."
Links: Other anti-British groups and Independent Israel groups, especially LEHI.
Status: Defunct.

Islamic Jihad

Principal area of operations: Middle East, Europe
Objectives: This is an anti-West group composed of Shi'ite fundamentalists. It first attracted large-scale publicity in April 1985 with the bombing of a Madrid restaurant. The attack killed eighteen people and wounded an additional 82 victims. Iran-funded Shi'ite groups operating under various banners have carried out several attacks in Europe. If there is any common objective behind such attacks, it is a fanatical hatred on the part of the perpetrators of anything which might pose a threat to the Ayatollah Khomeini in Iran.
Principal targets: U.S. military personnel and their

families and Americans.

Links: Other Shi'ite factions and governments supportive of the Ayatollah.

Status: Active.

JRA
Japanese Red Army

Principal area of operations: International

Objectives: This group first emerged in the 1960s as a coalition of extreme left-wing student groups. The group carried out various actions, predominantly hijackings, many of which were undertaken in support of, or as surrogate actions for, the PFLP, with whom they were closely linked. It was this group that perpetrated the Lod Airport massacre in 1972 which left some twenty-five people dead and seventy injured.

In the early 1980s, the group officially renounced terrorism as a weapon toward political change. There are continuing reports, however, that several JRA operatives are working with the PFLP in various capacities.

Principal targets: Japanese airlines and various pro-Israel targets. This group also enacted vicious punishment on its own members who had in some way transgressed the unwritten rules of JRA membership.

Links: PFLP, BR, Baader-Meinhof, PLO, and the governments of Libya and Cuba.

Status: Dormant/operational in a non-"front line" capacity.

Lebanese Armed Revolutionary Factions

Principal area of operations: Middle East, Europe

Objectives: This is an anti-Israeli/anti-"imperialist" group comprised in large part of Christians from villages in northern Lebanon. It is known to have many female members. It was this group that killed the United States military attaché in Paris in January 1982. Shortly afterward an Israeli diplomat was murdered with the same pistol, again in Paris. In 1984 the group killed another senior American official, in Rome.

Security forces were alerted to the structure of the group when an Arab courier, carrying explosives, was arrested in Spain. It was discovered that his passport contained several messages, written in Arabic and in code, which were to identify him to European supporters of the movement.

Links: Other anti-Israeli factions and the governments of Libya, Spain, and Iran.

Status: Active.

LEHI
Lohame Herut Israel
(The Stern Gang)

Principal area of operations: Palestine

Objectives: This was the most vicious and determined of the anti-British Israeli nationalist groups operating in Mandatory Palestine before, during, and following World War II. In 1939, the other major Israeli nationalist/separatist group, Irgun, suspended its activities; LEHI did not. In 1940, LEHI representatives approached both German and Italian officials in Beirut with a view to securing aid. Some four years later they also approached the Soviets.

Principal targets: British military personnel and "sympathizers," and anyone perceived as being against the establishment of an independent Israeli state.

Links: Irgun and the governments mentioned above.

Status: Defunct.

M19
Movimiento 19 Abril

Principal area of operations: Colombia

Objectives: This group was formed in 1973 following the failure of ANAPO (National Popular Alliance), a Colombian political party, to achieve power. Two of the party's supporters, Jaime Bateman Cayon and

Carlos Toledo Plata, decided that armed violence was the only way to achieve their aim of political power. During the 1970s, the group carried out various attacks and perpetrated several kidnaps. Toledo was captured in 1981. Like another Colombian terror group, FARC, M19 eventually established itself as a private army whose main task remains the protection of the cocaine barons operating in that country. M19 leaders at first accepted President Betancur's offer of an amnesty, but by July 1985 returned to their violent course.

Principal targets: Colombian government representatives and anyone who might pose a threat to the continuance of the cocaine trade.

Links: Other Colombian anti-government terrorist and guerrilla groups.

Status: Active.

MANO
Mano Blanca

Principal area of operations: Guatemala

Objectives: This was a right-wing group active in the 1960s. It established itself as a particularly vicious organization by sending pieces of murdered hostages to relatives with threatening letters.

Principal targets: Left-wing politicians and sympathizers of opposition left-wing terror groups.

Links: Other right-wing groups of the period.

Status: Defunct.

May Fifteenth Organization

Principal area of operations: Middle East, Europe

Objectives: This is a hard-line Palestinian "liberation" group.

Led by the shadowy Abu Ibrahim, this group is believed to be responsible for the failed attack on an El Al flight out of Heathrow Airport, London, in April 1986. In the April attempt, the pregnant girlfriend of an Ibrahim team member was used as an unwitting accomplice to carry a suitcase bomb on board the aircraft. Fortunately, it was discovered by El Al security personnel during a special preflight search.

The operation bears a striking similarity to earlier Ibrahim projects, with suitcase bombs and unwitting accomplices–young girls persuaded to accept "gifts" or engage in "smuggling" operations–being the common denominators. In one such incident in 1984, an Ibrahim bomb was successfully cleared through the Athens airport security checks and those at Tel Aviv by a girl who believed she was smuggling diamonds. The bomb was of a two-detonator type in which the first primes the second. Both detonators were designed to operate on the barometric principle (pressure); this should have resulted in the bomb exploding on the second leg of the flight from Athens to London via Tel Aviv. Ibrahim had hoped to give the impression that a terrorist cell was operational in Israel by having the bomb detonate in Israeli airspace.

The first detonator did its job: when the aircraft reached a certain height, it "tripped" and primed the second detonator. The second unit failed at the last moment, however, and the case was subsequently intercepted by British intelligence officers.

Ibrahim is a respected bomb technician, and his designs are continually becoming more sophisticated.

Links: Other Palestinian groups, and the governments of Syria, Libya, Iran, and the Soviet Union.

Status: Active.

MIR

Movimiento de la Izquierda Revolucionaria

Principal area of operations: Chile, Venezuela, Peru

Objectives: MIR was a left-wing movement most active in the late 1960s and early 70s. It coexisted with several other Latin American terror groups of various leftist ideologies and was a founder member of the Junta of Revolutionary Coordination.

Principal targets: Latin American diplomats at home and abroad, banks, and wealthy industrialists.

Links: Other left-wing groups of the period.

Status: Defunct.

MIRA
Movimiento Independista Revolucionario

Principal area of operations: Puerto Rico

Objectives: MIRA was a relatively small, left-wing nationalist/separatist group active in the 1960s.

Principal targets: Government politicians and diplomats, bars, and clubs. Some attacks have taken place in the U.S.

Links: FALN and other leftist groups.

Status: Defunct.

MLN
Movimiento de Liberacion Nacional
(Tupamaros)

Principal area of operations: Uruguay, Guatemala, Chile

Objectives: The Tupamaros were originally a leftist group formed in the early 1960s. Their intention was to establish an "alternative power." This attempt to mobilize the masses against the incumbent government was not as successful as the group hoped it might be. The various terrorist actions perpetrated by group members provoked an extremely hostile reaction from security forces as well as the more moderate left-wing political groups.

Principal targets: Initially, symbolic targets: office of the government, private businesses, etc. Foreign diplomats were eventually targeted, including American adviser Dan Mitrione, whom the group murdered. The attacks escalated to include military establishments and personnel.

Links: ALN, M19, Al-Fatah, and the governments of Libya and the Soviet Union.

Status: Dormant; absorbed into other movements. Some elements are operational under different banners.

MNR
Mozambique National Resistance (movement)

Principal area of operations: Mozambique

Objectives: This movement was originally sponsored to a large degree by Rhodesia and South Africa following the end of Portuguese rule in Africa in 1975. Both South Africa and Rhodesia were concerned that the left-wing government in Mozambique would attempt to spread its political ideologies at their expense. Operating under various banners, the MNR has been quite successful in undermining the Mozambique government and has also undertaken sporadic acts of sabotage in Zimbabwe. It is extremely doubtful that the South African authorities still exercise any great control over the MNR. The group is essentially anti-communist.

Principal targets: Mozambique regular forces and its supporters.

Links: Other African anti-communist groups, and the government of South Africa.

Status: Active.

Mohamed Boudia Commando
(Carlos Gang)

Principal area of operations: International

Objectives: "Carlos," whose real name is Illich Ramirez Sanchez, is a long-established figure in international terrorism. His most publicized operation took place in December 1975, in Vienna, when a gang stormed the OPEC building and kidnapped the representatives of several major oil-producing countries. It was widely publicized at the time that the raid had been sponsored to no small extent by Khadafi. Aside from the ransoms received by the gang for the safe release of the hostages, the only other concession the action achieved was the broadcast on Austrian radio of a left-wing ideological statement.

Principal targets: "Carlos," operating with any number of possible support teams, can be expected to strike against any target nominated by a sufficiently wealthy sponsor.

Links: The governments of Libya, the Soviet Union, and Cuba, and other international terrorist organizations.

Status: Active.

Montoneros
(Juan Jose Valle Montoneros)

Principal area of operations: Argentina

Objectives: The Montoneros were established in the 1960s. Their first major action was the kidnapping of ex-President Aramburu, whom they subsequently murdered in 1970. Like many other Latin American groups of the period, the Montoneros were leftist in outlook and supporters of the Peron regime.

Principal targets: Political figures from opposition groups and industrialists. The Montoneros hold the record for securing the highest ransom ever paid by a U.S. corporation. The sum, no less than sixty-one million dollars, was paid in 1974 for the release of Jorge and Juan Born, owners of the Bunge and Born grain exporting company. Sixty million dollars was paid in cash, and the additional one million dollars distributed to the "needy" in the form of clothing and food. A further condition of the release of the hostages was that the company erect busts of the late President Peron and his wife, Eva, in all their factories.

Links: Other Latin terror groups, the government of Libya, IRA, PLO, BR, TPLA, and ETA-M.

Status: Dormant; some elements operational under different banners.

NOA
Nueva Organizacion Anticomunista

Principal area of operations: Guatemala

Objectives: This was one of two main anti-communist/ right-wing groups established in Guatemala in the 1960s. In common with its sister organization, MANO, it adopted the technique of posting or hand-delivering pieces of a victim's body to its relatives and friends along with a warning message.

Principal targets: Communist sympathizers.

Links: MANO, other anti-communist/right wing groups.

Status: Defunct; some elements operational under different banners.

PAF
Protestant Action Front

Principal area of operations: Northern Ireland (Ulster)

Objectives: This is a loyalist Protestant group opposed completely to the unification of the Northern and Southern countries of Ireland. It is a particularly violent, paramilitary group which has claimed responsibility for the murders of several Catholics in Ulster.

Principal targets: Catholic members of the IRA factions or those perceived by the group as being in favor of a solution to the Irish problem which would result in the country being ruled from Dublin.

Links: Other Protestant paramilitary groups.

Status: Active.

PFLP
Popular Front for the Liberation of Palestine

Principal area of operations: International

Objectives: Formed in 1967 from various small terrorist groups and the Arab Nationalist Movement's Palestine Special Group for Armed Struggle, the PFLP is part of the PLO (Palestine Liberation Organization). It is a Marxist-Leninist movement opposed to any political settlement with Israel.

In the late 1970s, the PFLP split over policies and a breakaway group, the PFLP-Special Command, now led by Salim Abu Salim, adopted the overt terrorist path while the "official" PFLP renounced terrorism!

Principal targets: Any group, organization, or individual who is perceived by the group as being supportive of the Israeli regime and/or opposed to Marxist-Leninist ideologies.

Links: Other Palestinian terror groups; the governments of Libya, Algeria, United Arab Emirates, South Yemen, and the Soviet Union; and many other international terrorist organizations.

Status: The PFLP remains active under various banners.

PFLP-GC
Popular Front for the Liberation of Palestine, General Command

Principal area of operations: International

Objectives: This is another anti-Israeli Palestinian group. It was formed in 1968 from the PFLP Section B, itself an Ahmed Jibril Palestine Liberation Front splinter group. The group believes that too much time is wasted on political intercourse and favors aggressive action instead.

Principal targets: Same as those of the PFLP.

Links: Same as those of the PFLP, especially the governments of Libya and Syria, where many of its members are based.

Status: Active.

PLF
Palestine Liberation Front

Principal area of operation: Middle East, international

Objectives: The PLF is another member of the Rejectionist Front–the group of Palestinian organizations that oppose any form of political settlement with Israel. The PLF split from the PFLP-GC in 1977 because of the PFLP-GC's links with Lebanon and Syria.

Principal targets: Same as those of other Palestinian groups.

Links: Other Palestinian groups and the governments of Libya and Iraq. Many of its members are based in Baghdad.

Status: Active.

PLO
Palestine Liberation Organization

Principal area of operations: International

Objectives: An independent Palestinian state.

The PLO can be considered an umbrella organization that sponsors numerous Palestinian terror groups. Led by Yasser Arafat, the organization is at pains to distance itself from perpetrators of terror, preferring to give the impression of being a legitimate political group. This ongoing pattern of development was initiated by the Soviet Union (with which the PLO is inextricably linked) several years ago. So skillfully has the web of deception been woven that it would require a study far larger than this to document the growth and extension of this truly vast terrorist dynasty. Following is a selection of germane facts.

History: The PLO was officially formed in January 1964 at an Arab summit conference. By July 1966, Soviet involvement was established. In that year there was a meeting between Soviet Premier Aleksey Kosygin and Ahmad Shuquairy, then leader of the PLO. Shuquairy found disfavor with the Soviets, however, primarily because of his contacts with the Chinese. When he was overthrown in 1967, the Soviets were quick to criticize him, but not the organization.

In 1968, the Soviets launched an overt campaign of approval and justification for the Palestinian "partisans." Their intention was to isolate Israel and United States interests by exploiting the Arab-Israeli conflict. At this time, Yasser Arafat visited Moscow to negotiate arms supply and support details for joint psy-ops (psychological operations). Throughout this period, various Soviet embassies helped PLO elements, and the Jordanian Communist Party acted as an important link in the Moscow-Middle East chain.

By 1969, the PLO was established as an umbrella organization for several Palestinian terrorist groups. Moscow continued to justify PLO actions as the inevitable result of Israel's "provocations" and "adventurous" policies. On 28 February 1969, Pravda described the PLO attack on an El Al aircraft at Zurich as the action of "patriots defending their legal right to return to their homeland."

Defeat of the PLO forces in 1970 by forces loyal to King Hussein saw the dissolution of several Palestinian extremist factions and the absorption into the PLO of many more that were happy to accept Arafat as their leader.

By 1972, Soviet influence in the Middle East theater had begun to wane. This culminated in the Soviet delegation being expelled from Egypt by President Anwar Sadat. Loss of direct influence led to even wider use of the PLO by the Soviet Union as its political and military surrogate in the area. Increased fighting between the Arabs and Israelis, provoked by the Munich Olympic Games massacre of Israeli athletes, generated a renewed need on the part of the Arabs for weaponry. The Soviets were happy to provide this weaponry.

At about this time, the PLO and its sympathizers began a concerted effort to portray the organization as a nonterrorist group. All subsequent terrorist actions by PLO factions were denounced and/or disowned by them officially. The Soviet propaganda machine continues to play a major part in this exercise.

In 1974, this "legitimization" campaign peaked with the appearance of Yasser Arafat at the twenty-ninth General Assembly of the United Nations. Wearing a gun holster, he proclaimed at the Assembly his organization's intention to destroy the Israeli state, and he threatened continuance of terrorist attacks (carried out by other, less rational groups, of course) if his "peaceful" negotiations were not successful. A week later the PLO killed four Israeli civilians in an action at Bet Shan.

By 1975, "destruction" of Israel by the PLO had ceased to be a widely publicized ambition. The orgnization's aim was now proclaimed as the establishment of a Palestinian state within Israel. It was ultimately agreed at the twelfth PNC (Palestinian National Council) that claimed Palestinian territory would be accepted back from Israel on a stage-by-stage basis. In going along with this, Arafat showed a preparedness to compromise on the hard-line demands of earlier years. At the same time, the Soviets required that—even in the face of overwhelming evidence to the contrary—knowledge of Palestinian acts of terrorism, especially acts occurring outside the disputed areas, be denied by the PLO. The PLO was even to condemn these acts. It was this new moderation in the PLO that prompted the factional splits. Arafat's "reason" did not find favor with some of the extreme Palestinian elements. Despite attempts at reconciliation, such groups insisted that action, not words, was called for.

On 18 July 1980, Arafat was honored as a guest by Soviet leaders at the Moscow Olympics. From there he traveled to Managua, Nicaragua, where he was again accorded a hero's welcome by the Sandinista regime. The Sandinistas had reason to welcome the visit, as the PLO had for some time been helping to train Sandinista guerrillas.

The PLO's status as a legitimate political organization has continued to develop and mature. Regardless of official communiques and Soviet-inspired propaganda, the group still maintains close liaison with the vast majority, if not all, of the Palestinian terror groups. In 1982, the IDF (Israeli Defense Forces) in actions in Beirut, Tyre, and Sidon, captured documentary evidence of the PLO's role as an international terrorist umbrella movement. The documents also show a close relationship between the PLO and the KGB. It is clear that the use to the Soviets of the PLO has been great and will be greater as the sphere of PLO action continues to extend far beyond the Middle East. The threat from this quarter should not be underestimated.

PSF
Popular Struggle Front

Principal area of operations: Middle East

Objectives: This group was formed in Jordan in 1968. For a while it was a member of Al-Fatah but declared itself independent again at the end of the Arab-Israeli War in 1973. It is a little-heard-of group that is almost insignificant when compared to similar movements.

Principal targets: General Israeli-supportive targets.

Links: Tenuous links with other Palestinian groups and the governments of Libya and Iraq. Many of its members are based in Baghdad.

Status: Sporadically active.

RAF
Red Army Faction

Principal area of operations: West Germany, Europe

Objectives: The original RAF was an alliance of left-wing groups brought together by German activist lawyer Horst Mahler, following the Berlin student riots of 1968. The name was adapted from that of a Japanese terror group, the Japanese Red Army. The aims of the group were somewhat ambiguous, but were essentially anti-American, anti-bourgeois, and anarchic in nature. The group eventually adopted the names of its two most infamous leaders, Ulrike Meinhof and Andreas Baader, to become the Baader-

Meinhof (gang).

Following the demise of Meinhof and Baader, and the subsequent hunting down of RAF/Baader-Meinhof gang members by international police agencies, little was heard of the movement until the 1980s. At this time a new generation of terrorists using the RAF label appeared. Known in Germany as "The New Terrorists," these individuals are from various terror organizations–Fighting Communist Cells (Belgium), RAF (Germany) and Direct Action (France)–who are banding together to strike against common "enemies." These enemy targets are predominantly NATO military installations and the personnel connected with them. In much the same way that the Palestinian terror groups are currently engaging in joint offensives under a variety of banners, these left-wing European groups may appear and attack in the name of old movements or that of new ones.

Links: Fighting Communist Cells, Direct Action, IRA, PLO, PFLP, Black September, Red Brigade(s), and Armed Proletarian Cells (NAP).

Status: Active under this and various banners.

RZ
Revolutionary Zellen
(Red Cells)

Principal area of operations: West Germany

Objectives: This organization was established in West Germany in the mid-1970s. Members have attacked buildings and personnel infrequently during the last ten years. As the name suggests, it is a left-wing group but for some reason appears to have been excluded from the recently formed (1984) anti-NATO alliance of terror groups.

Principal targets: "Imperialists," businessmen, military personnel, and government offices.

Status: Sporadically active.

Saiqa
(As-Saiqa)

Principal area of operations: Middle East

Objectives: This movement was formed in October 1968 as the armed wing of the Vanguards of the Popular War for the Liberation of Palestine. This latter group had been established prior to the Arab-Israeli War of 1967 by elements of Syria's Ba'ath Party and the Syrian army's Palestine Battalion.

The group, being pro-Syrian, is opposed to the Iraqi-sponsored Rejectionist Front. It is an anti-Israel group.

Principal targets: This group has perpetrated relatively few, uninspired acts of terrorism. Its targets are those perceived as being Israeli-supportive/anti-Palestinian.

Links: Al-Fatah and other "moderate" Palestinian groups and the government of Syria.

Status: Sporadically active.

Sendero Luminoso
(Shining Path)

Principal area of operations: Peru

Objectives: The aims of this group are perhaps most simply described as the destabilization and overthrow of the existing Peruvian political system (which by comparison to many Latin American regimes is democratic). No specific aims are announced by the group, which combines guerrilla tactics and terrorism. Essentially, its ideology is Maoist/Marxist, but it professes no loyalty to existing Communist regimes. It has, in fact, attacked the embassies of both the United States and the Republic of China.

The Sendero Luminoso is named from a phrase in the writings of Jose Carlos Mariategui, founder of the Peruvian Communist Party, which says that the road to Communism is a "shining path." It is one of several groups currently operational in Peru. Many of these are a continuance of the Communist program initiated in South America and elsewhere in the 1960s. Elements of the ELN are believed to have crossed into Peru from neighboring Bolivia in the 1970s with a view to cooperation with existing Communist groups.

Links: Cuban support for some Peruvian groups is known to exist. There seems to be no firm evidence of the Sendero Luminoso having established international terror-group connections.

Status: Active.

17 November

Principal area of operations: Greece

Objectives: This is a left-wing group opposed to the existing Greek regime and "capitalists" in general. The name of the group is taken from the date on which students rose up in revolt against the former military regime in Greece, leading ultimately to its downfall.

The group authenticates its operations—which for the most part have been extremely professional political assassinations of Greeks and Americans—by leaving leaflets at the site of the incident.

Links: Other left-wing terror groups in Europe and elsewhere.

Status: Active.

SWAPO
South West African Peoples Organization

Principal area of operations: Southern and South West Africa

Objectives: SWAPO was established in 1960 as an expansion and development of the Ovamboland Peoples Organization. It is a left-wing group which seeks to implement a system of "democratic socialism" in Namibia (a South African controlled area of South West Africa). Despite claims to the contrary by the organization's spokesmen, the group is most certainly inclined toward terrorist action.

Principal targets: SA government "sympathizers" and others who oppose the movement's left-wing ideologies, and South African security force personnel.

Links: The governments of Angola and Cuba, and other Southern African left wing groups.

Status: Active.

TPLA
Turkish People's Liberation Army

Principal area of operations: Turkey

Objectives: This left-wing group was formed from various extremist groups of students. Especially active in the early 1970s, the group provided a right-wing backlash, and a wave of left-wing vs. right-wing battles spread across the country. In 1980, a military coup ended the steadily escalating political wars and over the next few months some forty thousand people—neo-Fascist and Communist alike—were arrested and imprisoned.

Principal targets: Right-wing group members.

Links: Other leftist groups in Turkey; ETA, PLO, IRA, BR, and others.

Status: Dormant; sporadically active.

UDA
Ulster Defense Association

Principal area of operations: Northern Ireland (Ulster)

Objectives: The UDA was formed in 1971 in opposition to the IRA. The group is now the largest and most powerful Protestant paramilitary force in the province. It has sympathizers in the police and the Ulster Defense Regiment. It opposes the idea of power-sharing with the South and is determined to keep the North securely coupled with mainland Britain.

Principal targets: IRA sympathizers and Catholics (primarily "revenge" attacks.)

Links: Other Protestant groups.

Status: Active.

UFF
Ulster Freedom Fighters

Principal area of operations: Northern Ireland (Ulster)

Objectives: This group is an extreme breakaway movement whose members were once UDA operatives. Established in 1973, the UFF are particularly violent. Like other Protestant groups in Ireland, they oppose the idea of unification of Northern Ireland and Ireland.

Principal targets: Catholic/IRA targets, individuals, and business interests.

Links: Other Protestant groups–including the UDA (although both groups deny this).

Status: Active.

UVF
Ulster Volunteer Force

Principal area of operations: Northern Ireland (Ulster)

Objectives: This is another Protestant group opposed to unification with the South. It was formed in 1966 as a movement to oppose the IRA. It has employed terrorist techniques in the past, although the group officially denounces terrorism.

Principal targets: IRA supporters.

Links: Other Protestant para-military groups.

Status: Active.

Bibliography

Arendt, H. *On Revolution.* New York: Penguin, 1965.

Arendt, H. *On Violence.* New York: Harcourt, Brace and World, 1969.

Asprey, Robert B. *War in the Shadows: The Guerrilla in History.* New York: Doubleday, 1975.

Barnet, Richard. *Intervention and Revolution.* London: Granada, 1972.

Barron, John. *KGB: The Secret Work of Soviet Secret Agents.* New York: Corgi, 1975.

Bell, J. B. *Transnational Terror.* Washington, D.C.: American Enterprise Institute for Public Policy Research, 1975.

Bell, J. B. *Terror Out of Zion: Irgun Zvai Leumi and the Palestine Underground 1929–1949.* New York: Avon, 1977.

Bell, J. B. *A Time of Terror.* New York: Basic Books, 1978.

Bittman, L. *The Deception Game.* New York: Ballantine, Espionage Intelligence Library, 1972.

Brock, G., et al. *Siege.* London: The Observer, 1980.

Burns, A. *The Angry Brigade.* London: Quartet Books, 1974.

Burton, A. *Urban Terrorism: Theory, Practice and Response.* New York: The Free Press, 1975.

Camus, A. *The Rebel.* Harmondsworth, England: Penguin, 1962.

Carlton, D. *International Terrorism and World Security.* London: Croom Helm, 1975.
Carr, E. H. *Karl Marx: A Study in Fanaticism.* London: J. M. Dent and Sons, 1934.
Carr, E. H. *Studies in Revolution.* New York: Grosset and Dunlap, 1964.
Chapman, B. *Police State.* New York: Praeger, 1970.
Clutterbuck, R. *Living with Terrorism.* London: Faber and Faber, 1975.
Clutterbuck, R. *Britain in Agony: The Growth of Political Violence.* London: Faber and Faber, 1978.
Clutterbuck, R. *Kidnap and Ransom: The Response.* London: Faber and Faber, 1978.
Connor, M. *Duty Free: Smuggling Made Easy.* Boulder, Colorado: Paladin Press, 1983.
Connor, M. *How to Hide Anything.* Boulder, Colorado: Paladin Press, 1984.
Connor, M. *Sneak It Through: Smuggling Made Easier.* Boulder, Colorado: Paladin Press, 1984.
Conquest, R. *The Nation Killers: The Deportation of Nationalities.* London: Macmillan, 1970.
Conquest, R. *Lenin.* Glasgow: Fontana/Collins, 1972.
Coogan, T. *The IRA.* London: Fontana, 1980.
Debray, R. *Revolution in a Revolution.* Harmondsworth, England: Penguin, 1968.
Debray, R. *Strategy for Revolution.* Harmondsworth, England: Penguin, 1973.
Demaris, O. *Brothers in Blood: The International Terrorist Network.* New York: Scribner, 1977.
Deriabin, P. *Watchdogs of Terror: Russian Bodyguards from the Tsars to the Commissars.* New York: Arlington House, 1972.
Dobson, C. *Black September.* London: Hale, 1975.
Dobson, C. and Payne, R. *The Carlos Complex.* London: Hodder and Stoughton, 1977.
Dobson, C. and Payne, R. *The Weapons of Terror.* London: Macmillan, 1979.
Francis, S. T. *The Soviet Strategy of Terror.* Washington, D.C.: The Heritage Foundation, 1981.

Freeman, C. *Terrorism.* London: Batsford Academic and Educational, 1981.

Fugua, P. and Wilson, J.V. *Terrorism: The Executive's Guide to Survival.* Houston: Gulf Publishing Company, 1978.

Gibson, B. *The Birmingham Bombs.* London: Barry Rose, 1976.

Great Britain: *Report of the Committee of Inquiry into Police Interrogation Procedures in Northern Ireland.* London: HMSO, 1979.

Guevara, C. *Guerrilla Warfare.* Harmondsworth, England: Penguin, 1969.

Halperin, E. *Terrorism in Latin America.* Washington, D.C.: Sage, 1976.

Hammond, T.T. *The Anatomy of Communist Takeovers.* New Haven: Yale Univ. Press, 1975.

Hanley, D. *The Art of Imperialism.* San Francisco: n.p., 1985.

Hayes, D. *Terrorists and Freedom Fighters.* Hove, EnGland: Wayland, 1980.

Hoare, M. *Mercenary.* London: Transworld (Corgi), 1978.

Horowitz, I. L. *The Anarchists.* New York: Dell, 1964.

Hyams, E. *Terrorists and Terrorism.* London: J.M. Dent and Sons, 1975.

Jackson, G. *People's Prison.* London: Faber and Faber, 1973.

Johnson, K. *Guatemala: From Terrorism to Terror.* London: Institute for Study of Conflict, 1972.

Kahn, D. *Hitler's Spies.* New York: Macmillan, 1978.

Kitson, F. *Low Intensity Operations.* London: Faber and Faber, 1971.

Laqueur, W. *Terrorism.* London: Weidenfield and Nicolson, 1977.

Lee, D. and Pratt, C. *Operation Julie.* London: W.H. Allen and Co., 1978.

Liston, R. *Terrorism.* New York: Thomas Nelson, 1977.

Long, D. *Chemical/Biological Warfare Survival.* Wamego, Kansas: Long Survival Pubs., 1980.

McConnell, B. *Assassination.* London: Leslie Frewin, 1969.

McKnight, G. *The Mind of the Terrorist.* London: Michael Joseph, 1974.

Marighella, C. *For the Liberation of Brazil.* Harmondsworth, England: Penguin, 1971.

Marighella, C. *Mini-Manual of the Urban Guerrilla.* Boulder, Colorado: Paladin Press, 1986.

Meguire, P. G. and Kramer, J. J. *Psychological Deterrents to Nuclear Theft: A Preliminary Literature Review and Bibliography.* Washington, D.C.: U.S. Dept. of Commerce, 1976.

Moore, K. C. *Airport, Aircraft and Airline Security.* Los Angeles: Security World, 1976.

Moss, R. *Urban Guerrillas.* London: Temple Smith, 1972.

Parry, A. *Terrorism from Robespierre to Arafat.* New York: Vanguard, 1976.

Pincher, C. *The Secret Offensive.* London: Sidgwick and Jackson, 1985.

Phillips, D. *Skyjack.* London: Harrap, 1973.

Pipes, R. *Russia under the Old Regime.* Harmondsworth, England: Penguin, 1979.

Powell, W. *The Anarchist's Cookbook.* Boulder, Colorado: Paladin Press, 1985.

Shaw, J., et al. *Ten Years of Terrorism: Collected Views.* New York: Crane, Russak, 1979.

Skolnick, J. H. *The Politics of Protest.* New York: Ballantine, 1969.

Santoro, V. *Disruptive Terrorism.* Port Townsend, Washington: Loompanics, 1984.

Stevenson, W. *Ninety Minutes to Entebbe.* London: Corgi, 1977.

Thomas, H. *The Spanish Civil War.* Harmondsworth, England: Penguin, 1979.

Tinnin, D. *Hit Team.* London: Weidenfield and Nicolson, 1976.

Tokes, R. L. *Dissent in the USSR.* Baltimore: John Hopkins Univ. Press, 1975.

Tolstoy, N. *Stalin's Secret War.* London: Jonathon Cape, 1981.

Trotsky, L. *Terrorism and Communism.* Ann Arbor, Michigan: Ann Arbor Paperbacks, 1920.

Trotsky, L. *The Defence of Terrorism.* London: Allen and Unwin, 1921.

Trotsky, L. *Against Individual Terrorism.* New York: Pathfinder Press, 1974.

Vigor, P.H. *The Soviet View of War, Peace and Neutrality.* London: Routledge, 1975.

Walzer, M. *Just and Unjust Wars.* Harmondsworth, England: Penguin, 1980.

Wilkinson, P. *Political Terrorism.* London: Macmillan, 1977.

Wilkinson, P. *Terrorism and the Liberal State.* London: Macmillan, 1977.

Wilkinson, P. *The New Fascists.* London: Grant McIntyre, 1981.

Wilkinson, P. *British Perspectives on Terrorism.* London: Allen and Unwin, 1981.

Will, I. *The Big Brother Society.* London: Harrap, 1983.

Wolin, S. and Slusser, R.M. *The Soviet Secret Police.* London: Methuen, 1957.

Index